Where's Your Jesus Now? is heartbreaking and witty, full of compassion and righteous outrage. It's a fascinating book.

A. J. JACOBS
Author of *The Year of Living Biblically*

Karen Zacharias has testified! This book is funny, fierce, and fearless. My stomach hurts from laughing, and my heart aches from finding the truth.

DOUG CRANDELL
Author of *Hairdos of the Mildly Depressed*
and *The Flawless Skin of Ugly People*

Poignant, funny, and cutting edge, *Where's Your Jesus Now?* breaks new ground and knocks fundamentalist thought on its rear.

MICHAEL MORRIS
Author of *Slow Way Home*

If Karen Spears Zacharias should turn evangelist, the stadium will be full every night.

SONNY BREWER
Author of *The Poet of Tolstoy Park*

Karen Spears Zacharias craves the Jesus of Hank Williams, Thomas Jefferson, Blind Willie Johnson, and William Blake. In essays bristling with doubt and fear, buoyed by flashes of the brightest hope and splashes of the darkest humor, she grants us the privilege of joining her search party. She almost — almost! — has me convinced He's out there somewhere.

JACK PENDARVIS
Author of *Awesome* and
Your Body Is Changing

Candid as all get-out, Karen Spears Zacharias knows where Jesus is. In this essential work she prods us from our comfort zone and — mercifully — transports us straight into His arms.

SALLY JOHN
Author of A *Time to Mend*
and other novels

The wit and wisdom of Karen Spears Zacharias spoken in a clear, no-holds-barred voice creates a book to be pondered and enjoyed.

JACKIE K. COOPER
Author of *The Bookbinder*

With wit and common sense, *Where's Your Jesus Now?* calls us to live our Christian faith without fear. Karen Spears Zacharias reminds us that if we truly have faith, what should we fear?

W. RALPH EUBANKS
Author of *Ever Is a Long Time:
A Journey into Mississippi's Dark Past*

Witty, brave, and bold, Zacharias dares to ask the tough question for the right reason: to affirm that Jesus is far more than many of his fear-driven followers believe He is. In a world that has cheapened God, this is the right book at the right time. It cuts to the cultural chase like the words of Brennan Manning and Oswald Chambers, challenging us while encouraging us. And Zacharias does so with a humble heart, a discerning pair of eyes, and an engaging style. *Where's Your Jesus Now?* has the power to change the way we all look at God. This is not only a good book, it's the most important book I've read in years.

BOB WELCH
award-winning author,
columnist and speaker

WHERE'S YOUR JESUS NOW?

WHERE'S YOUR JESUS NOW?

EXAMINING HOW FEAR ERODES OUR FAITH

Karen Spears Zacharias

ZONDERVAN®

ZONDERVAN.com/
AUTHORTRACKER
follow your favorite authors

ZONDERVAN®

Library of Congress Cataloging-in-Publication Data

Zacharias, Karen Spears.
     Examining how fear erodes our faith / Karen Spears Zacharias.
        p. cm.
     ISBN 978-0-310-28386-7 (hardcover)
     1. Fear — Religious aspects — Christianity. I. Title.
BV4908.5.Z33   2008
248.8'6 — dc22   2008007376

Interior design by Beth Shagene

Printed in the United States of America

08 09 10 11 12 13 • 21 20 19 18 17 16 15 14 13 12 11 10 9 8 7 6 5 4 3 2 1

For Shirley Dunham,
Agnes Ferngren, and Connie Henricks.

≪ ≫

Women who knew.

Contents

Night of TERROR

ERIC SHANNON WAS A RELIGIOUS MAN. RAISED UP BAPTIST, he believed in the virgin birth, the crucifixion, and the resurrection of Jesus Christ. He also believed in water baptism, the Trinity of God, and the Ten Command-ments. For a time, Eric felt God was calling him into the ministry as a pastor.

His mother, Shirley Dunham, recalled that as a teen-ager, her son "was a little evangelist. He knew his Bible very well."

But somewhere along the way, Eric grew dissatis-fied with the washed-in-the-blood-of-the-Lamb version of Christianity that his mother had instilled in him. He wanted to claim a faith of his own. When it came time to raise his own family, Eric settled on a perversion of Judaism. Eric fathered seven children, four daughters and three sons. He made it clear that his children were not allowed to question his authority — ever. They were taught to obey their father. And to fear him.

Shirley, an old-fashioned Baptist, didn't much care for the way Eric was raising her grandchildren. She wasn't sure where he'd gone astray, but there was no question he had. The two argued bitterly about their conflicting beliefs.

Eric became obsessed with Levitical law. He rejected the message of the New Testament — the foundational cornerstone of his mother's faith — altogether. He wouldn't allow his children to attend public school because he feared they would be given hot dogs for lunch, a direct violation of Eric's no-pork rule.

Eric embraced a primogenitor philosophy held by many traditional societies — a belief that a family's eldest son is to be honored above all others. He taught his eldest son, only thirteen, that he had, by birthright, dominion over his younger siblings, particularly his sisters. This was all part of God's order for man, Eric insisted. Handing over his belt to his boy, Eric encouraged him to whip his sisters if they didn't do whatever he ordered. The boy protested, but enjoyed the honor of being his father's chosen son.

Eric's oldest daughter told no one of the abuse she suffered at the hands of her father. But the eleven-year-old kept track of that abuse in a worn journal that chronicled her family's history. She wrote of beatings, obscenities, drugs, and sex. She was sure of one thing: If her father ever found out what she was writing, he'd kill her.

The frightened girl told her grandmother that her

father had repeatedly threatened her. Shirley recalled her son's threat: "Eric told the kids that he put them in this world and that he could take them out." Shirley knew that Eric wasn't spouting off in a good-natured way. He meant what he said. Literally.

Seeking help the only way she deemed safe, Eric's daughter gave her dangerous diary to Shirley, who, after much deliberation and with much unease, turned it over to Oregon's Department of Human Services.

The diary provided the state agency with a detailed account of times that Eric withheld food from his kids and offered them marijuana instead. While other kids were watching Disney flicks, Eric's children were treated to a steady fare of pornography. He cuffed his kids around quite a bit. Some nights the kids would huddle together in the back seat of the family's car while Eric's common-law wife, the mother of the youngest four children, Robin Hocker, earned money as a dancer in a strip joint.

Eric's fundamentalist beliefs gave him the one thing he was searching for — justification. With God on his side, who could stand against him? Eric felt it was his right to intimidate others. He did so without fear of retaliation or repercussions because God was his defender. It was Eric and God against the world. Eric trusted no one, particularly not anyone affiliated with any government agencies.

His mother knew there would be hell to pay when the state agency removed the children from Eric and Robin and placed them in her care. Shirley warned agency officials that they were in way over their heads.

One afternoon, the phone rang. It was Eric, screaming at his mother, "Give me my children back, or I'll come and kill you!"

It was a promise. Not a threat.

Shortly after ten o'clock on a chilly Wednesday night — prayer meeting night — in January of 1998, Eric Shannon and Robin Hocker pulled into the drive of Charles and Shirley Dunham's rural trailer house. Eric reached across the front seat for his gun — an SKS. He told his pregnant partner, Robin, to grab the other guns — a .22 and a 12-gauge shotgun — along with some extra ammunition. Carrying the loaded weapons, they walked in hushed silence to the south side of the Dunhams' yard, where Eric cut the phone lines.

He removed a screen from a window, climbed into the living room, and opened the front door for Robin. The couple's three-year-old son was asleep on the couch.

Brandishing the semi-automatic assault rifle, Eric barreled into his mother's bedroom, demanding that she hand over his firstborn son.

"Give me my son!" he screamed.

Shirley tried to tell him she didn't know where the eldest boy was. Suspecting that Eric might use force to reclaim the boy, the state agency had placed him with a foster family in a nearby town. Eric cursed his mother.

In the past, Robin had acted as a peacemaker between Shirley and Eric, but not that night. Robin, eight months pregnant with Eric's child, pulled a gun on Shirley.

<< >>

"That night she was completely helping him," Shirley said in an interview at her home a year afterward. The wrinkles in her forehead and around her eyes deepened in recollection. "I had my hand on the barrel of the gun. I tried to wrestle it away from her, but she kept shoving me back. If I had gotten it, Eric probably would've killed me."

Eric pulled the butt of his rifle up to his shoulder, jumped across the bed, and threatened his mother as she and Robin struggled down the hall. Shirley's husband, Charles Dunham, muscled his way between Eric and Shirley.

"I can't let you shoot your mom," Charles said. Eric pushed the SKS into his stepdad's gut. Charles knocked the barrel away. Eric pulled the trigger, shooting Charles in the thigh, blowing off all the flesh. Bone shattered. Blood gushed.

"Dad's shot Grandpa!" Shirley's eldest granddaughter screamed.

"Mommy, you got a gun? Daddy's here? You got guns?" a wide-eyed toddler asked.

Scooping the three-year-old up in her arms, Shirley started for the door. Robin raised the gun at Shirley.

"Put my baby down, or I'll blow you away," Robin demanded.

Shirley obeyed. Robin pushed Shirley back down the hallway at gunpoint. While Charles lay bleeding on the floor, Eric apologized to his stepfather and his mother, then he ordered his mother to be tied up.

"One minute Eric was saying he was sorry for what

he'd done," Charles said. "The next he was stomping on my leg and screaming at me to tell him where his boy was. I didn't know where the boy was."

Shirley had been hog-tied and was on the bed. Robin straddled Shirley and pressed the gun's barrel against Shirley's chest. Noting a painting of Jesus hanging on the wall above the bed, Robin taunted her.

"Where's your Jesus now?" Robin asked.

"He's right here," Shirley replied.

"You really believe that?"

"Yes, I do," Shirley answered firmly.

Robin laughed.

Eric yelled at Robin to get all the kids into the car. Robin left the bound-up grandmother on the bed. She began to put shoes and coats on the kids, but Eric told her to forget it. Robin, her rapid breath visible in the cold night air, herded five children into the backseat of the car, covering them under a sleeping bag. Before leaving, Eric shot out the tires on the Dunhams' vehicles. He hopped into the passenger seat and ordered Robin to get a move on it.

<< >>

Oregon State Police Sergeant Dale Breshears, a twenty-two-year veteran of the force, said "God's fate" guided him the night Eric Shannon and Robin Hocker kidnapped their children at gunpoint. An all-call woke him around 10:30 p.m. A police chase was underway. The suspect was shooting. A unit was down. There was no mention of any children.

Breshears didn't take time to wash up. He dressed and reached for the mouthwash. After a quick gargle, he was out the door.

His shotgun, which he'd grabbed from police headquarters, was loaded with three rounds of double-ought buckshot and one slug, an old habit of his. The dispatcher said the suspect's vehicle was headed east on the freeway. Breshears assumed all the action would be over by the time he arrived.

<< >>

Police officials from every law enforcement agency in Oregon's Umatilla County were in pursuit of Eric Shannon and Robin Hocker. They did not know about the children crouching in the backseat. The police followed in blackout formation — no lights flashing, no headlights. If Eric spotted a light, he fired at it. Rounds from his assault rifle skipped off the pavement like ashes flicked from a cigarette. The report drowned out the radio frequency. One bullet struck a police car.

"Forty-nine, twenty-three, you're smoking badly," a Hermiston police officer said.

The state trooper kept driving.

<< >>

Pendleton police officer Shane Hagey was checking someone into detox when the first call for assistance came through. As the chase moved closer to Pendleton, Hagey headed out to help.

State police were placing a tack strip at exit 207, the

airport exit. Officer Hagey pulled his unit horizontally across an exit to the city in an effort to block Eric's car. As he pulled his unit up, Hagey could hear the pop of gunfire. The caravan of police cars stretching out before him looked otherworldly.

"It seemed like I could see police cars forever," Hagey recalled.

The tack strip deflated the front tires of the car upon impact. Robin wanted to stop, but Eric screamed at her to keep driving. Leaning out the window again, he fired off another.

"Get back!" he shouted.

Driving on rims with sparks flying, Robin screamed, "Can I pull over here?"

Eric offered no reply, no protest.

She swung the disabled car to the right, toward the BP station at Pendleton's Indian Hills. A line of police cars followed.

<< >>

I drove past Sergeant Breshears as he charged up the hill toward the BP station. My boss, the editor of the *East Oregonian*, had called me at home twenty minutes earlier. There was a police pursuit underway, he said. I was a general assignment reporter, but law enforcement was my beat.

"You better hurry," he'd ordered.

Up until that night I'd never heard of Eric Shannon or Robin Hocker. I didn't know Shirley Dunham or her husband Charles. And I knew nothing of the telling diary or the nightmares that compelled a frightened girl to write it.

I whipped my car into the parking lot at the Red Lion Inn, directly across the road from the gas station. Grabbing the only weapons I carried — a notebook and pen — I rushed toward the action. A local officer waved to me, offering me shelter behind the passenger door of his unit. I gladly accepted.

<< >>

Police cars circled the convenience mart from all sides. Sergeant Breshears knew there were two employees at the gas station — one working the pumps and one inside at the counter. Breshears carried a shotgun and his service revolver. Officer Hagey joined Sergeant Breshears. A red pickup parked near a north fence provided cover for the two of them. They were within thirty feet of a very agitated Eric Shannon.

Eric exited the car, swinging his guns, shouting obscenities, demanding to know where his boy was. He assumed a combat-mode position, moving his rifle back and forth. Robin climbed out of the car. A line of kids followed.

The police held their fire.

"Look at all those kids," one stunned officer said.

Sergeant Breshears tunneled in on Eric's assault rifle. "I was watching, focused on Eric's car and the front door of the store," Breshears explained. "I was thinking about one thing — that assault rifle. It's designed for one purpose. To kill people."

Eric yelled at Robin to get the keys, the shotgun, and the backpacks. She panicked. "I was scared," she said in an interview from prison a year later. "I picked up my youngest boy. I picked him up for cover because I didn't want to be shot."

Clutching the two-year-old in front of her as a human shield, Robin turned back to the car while the eleven-year-old daughter hustled her siblings past a ranting Eric into the store. They huddled in the center aisle along with the store's clerk.

<< >>

Outside, Officer Hagey couldn't get those children out of his mind. The young father was new to law enforcement, and most of his police activity to this point had consisted of controlling barking dogs and obnoxious drunks.

Broad of shoulder and as finely chiseled as an NFL running back, Hagey dropped to his belly and crawled up under the truck. That's when Robin, collecting equipment from the car, spotted him and Sergeant Breshears in the dark. Both were so close that Robin felt she could whisper to them.

"I wish all the time I'd run for that one cop I saw lying on the ground, waiting," she said later. But unsure of who would shoot her first if she made a run for it — the cops or Eric — Robin grabbed the guns and ammo and made a mad dash for the store.

Hagey crawled out from underneath the truck. Sergeant Breshears scanned the situation. "We've got to take him out," he told Hagey. "Do you see him? Do you see him?"

Eric followed Robin into the store. Kneeling behind the counter, he raised the rifle like he was taking sight, but he didn't shoot. Perhaps the glaring overhead lights made it impossible for him to see into the darkness where all the officers waited, guns aimed, ready to fire.

Every officer noticed the crazed look in Eric's eyes minutes later as he came back out of the store.

"He came out of that store with a purpose. He was a man on a mission," one officer recalled.

Breshears and Hagey held their breath as Eric dropped on one knee and aimed his gun. He continued to holler, "What have you done with my son? What have you done with my son?"

Boom! Boom! Both officers fired at the same time. A barrage of gunfire followed — a total of eight rounds in a split second.

A slug from a state trooper's gun struck Eric below the right armpit, puncturing his lung, nicking his spine. The buckshot from Sergeant Breshears's gun caused superficial cuts to Eric's trigger finger. Officer Hagey was unaware that his gun was loaded with four-shot — totally ineffective to stop a threat.

Momentarily stunned, Eric reached for his gun, which had been jarred from his grip. Hagey fired off a second round. Glass went flying. He chambered the round for a third shot, but before he got it off, Sergeant Breshears fired off his second and third round of buckshot. Then he fired the gun's lone slug, striking Eric in the head.

"They're killing my dad!" the young girl shrieked.

Eric Shannon collapsed. Dead at age thirty-three.

Police swarmed the store, taking Robin into custody and the children into protective care.

Later Eric's eldest daughter told her grandparents, "I prayed for God to kill my daddy. I guess he did."

<< >>

I watched with unease as someone covered Eric's body.

I'd been at murder scenes, fatal car crashes, and deadly fires. I'd seen the body of a drunk, bloated and discolored, floating downstream in the Umatilla River in broad daylight, and the blue and bruised body of my own father as he was shipped home under protection of Plexiglas from the steamy jungles of South Vietnam, but I had never actually been an eyewitness to such violence before that chilling January night.

Who were these people? Who had taken Eric Shannon's son? And why? What just happened? Were my kids still safe in bed? Was this a local family? Had I seen them at ball games or choir concerts?

A year later, I visited Robin Hocker at the Eastern Oregon Correctional Facility. She was only twenty-six years old when her children were taken by the courts into protective custody and she was sent to prison.

Fear, she claimed, was the undercurrent of her poor choices. Numerous friends and loved ones had urged her to leave Eric, to seek refuge at a domestic shelter, but she was too afraid.

"Nobody left Eric without his permission. Whenever

I tried, he threatened to take my life, the lives of our children, and the lives of my family."

As prison doors clinked around us, Robin leaned forward, clasped her hands as if in prayer, and said, "I lived in a fear I didn't need to be living in. I thought Eric was invincible; he wasn't. Had I walked away, I would be in a better situation today. The hundred times I walked away, I should have stayed away, but I was too afraid."

Her choices have cost her more than just time served. Robin Hocker lost the one thing she believed she was protecting — her kids.

I also visited Charles and Shirley Dunham in their rural Oregon home, where they were raising the baby born after Eric Shannon died, and a sister. The two youngest boys lived in Washington state. They'd been adopted by Eric's brother Jeff and his wife. Eric's older three children — including the boy he sought that night — had been sent by children services to Kansas to live with their biological mother.

Prior to marrying Charles Dunham, Shirley said she'd been in an abusive relationship, so she had an inclination as to why Robin did what she did. As a Christian, Shirley felt strongly that divorce was wrong. She stayed with her abuser but was relieved when he finally left her, even though that meant raising four boys on her own.

Victims of domestic violence need to find the courage to step out and get help, Shirley said, "otherwise the abuser will continue to scare them into coming back."

The way her ex-husband did. The way Eric did Robin.

"Fear can make you do a lot of things you don't think you'd do," Shirley said. "As a mother, I can't believe Robin would deliberately put her children at risk, but she did. She had a loaded gun. And she mocked me about being a Christian."

I asked her what she thought went wrong with the son who once felt the call to be a preacher.

"Eric took from the Bible only the parts that suited him," Shirley said. He used Scriptures primarily as a justification for his actions and for his attitude toward the law, toward his family, and toward the nation. "After converting to Mormonism, Eric decided I was going to hell because I didn't believe the way he did," Shirley recalled. Then, when Mormonism lost its luster, Eric studied to become a Buddhist, and that was followed by a conversion to his own jumble of Judaism.[1]

Eric was obviously a man on a spiritual quest.

Charles Dunham has undergone five surgeries to repair the damage caused by the gunshot wound he received that night. Yet he harbors no anger toward his dead stepson. "It's been an overwhelming thing to take all that has happened to try and deal with as a family. It's a tough go," Charles said. "But where do you end all the hostilities and try and heal all that has happened?"

Eric had religion up the yin-yang, but it did not bring him one iota of comfort or sensibility. Without pause, Eric could quote line and verse Scriptures about Jesus, but he did not know the Jesus C. S. Lewis wrote about:

God could, had he pleased, have been incarnate in a man of iron nerves, the stoic sort who lets no sigh escape him. Of his great humility, he chose to be incarnate in a man of delicate sensibilities who wept at the grave of Lazarus and sweated blood at Gethsemane. Otherwise we should have missed the great lesson that it is by his *will* alone that man is good or bad, and that feelings are not, in themselves, of any importance. We should also have missed the all-important help of knowing that he has faced all that the weakest of us face, has shared not only the strength of our nature, but every weakness of it, except sin. If he had been incarnate in a man of immense courage, that would have been for many of us almost the same as his not being incarnate at all.[2]

In his paranoia-fueled fervor, Eric Shannon went in search of a God of retribution, and he missed the God of redemption altogether. But Eric isn't the only one who has been waylaid by fear and despair. Lately it seems far too many of us are inclined to exploit faith as Eric did, relying on it as justification to disdain, dismiss, and destroy others. I've done it. You've probably done it too.

Charles' question is a good one, though. Where should we go to put an end to all the wrongs and try to heal all that has happened?

To none other than the Jesus who wept at the gravesite.

Feasting on FEAR

I HAVE ALWAYS BELIEVED THERE WAS MORE TO ERIC Shannon than what I reported in the newspaper. I imagine that, at some point, Eric was a good brother, that he cared for his siblings, his children, and, yes, even his mother.

How can it be that a man who has spent countless hours poring over Scriptures, searching with due diligence for life's deeper meaning, comes up shorthanded with a loaded gun?

That vision of Eric shooting his stepfather at point-blank range, apologizing profusely the next minute, only to stomp repeatedly on Charles' leg a moment later is a troubling image, one that I fear reflects my own irrational behavior at times. Do you suppose my actions leave God as confused and distraught as Eric's did those who loved him?

Somewhere just north of Nashville, there lives a young

mother suffering from an ulcer. The underlying cause of her condition is fear. She lives in a cul-de-sac in a town bordering a military base. The cul-de-sac, she explained, provides more security than other neighborhoods because a person can see who is coming and going.

Among her biggest concerns is that her son's school will be attacked by terrorists. I asked why she would even entertain such an idea, and she pointed to the 2004 school shooting in Russia as the source of her worries.

The Beslan School massacre resulted in the deaths of 341 people, including 186 children, and the wounding of hundreds of others, some severely. More than 1,200 adults and children were captured in the attack. For three days, people worldwide tuned their television channels toward the drama in Russia. We are gawkers by nature, crows squawking over roadkill, rubberneckers pausing to see the wreck. But we stop, in part, because we care. We want to know, is there any way we can help? Believers around the world were moved to pray for the hostages and their families.[1]

What motivated the bloodbath remains a matter of debate. Some, like this mother, believe the official Russian assertion that the attack was the work of terrorists. Others disavow the government's claim that the perpetrators were terrorists linked to al-Qaeda. They say such allegations are political posturing, intended to divert attention from the real culprits — Chechen separatists.[2]

But what's all that got to do with an elementary school in Tennessee?

"I can't think of anywhere else terrorists are more apt

to strike at the heart of Americans than an elementary school near a military base," the mom said.

I sat in stunned silence as she continued to explain that as a God-fearing Christian woman, she wholeheartedly supported the decision to invade Iraq.

"Do you know what the insurgents do to the bodies of dead children?" she asked. "They stuff bombs into their bodies, so that when their parents or authorities, or our soldiers go to retrieve them, they are blown up too."

We had to invade Iraq, she insisted; otherwise, al-Qaeda would surely bring the fight to our own little cul-de-sacs, obliterating any illusions we might have about living in safe neighborhoods.

Never mind that the 9/11 Commission concluded there was no connection between Iraq and the terrorists responsible for 9/11. Or the fact that it was our own runaway fears, coupled with poor intelligence and even shoddier reporting, that got us into the war.

"Iraq," she added, "is the seventh ring of hell. There is so much evil over there."

Good thing we live over here, in the lap of one nation under God and at the mercy and good pleasure of oil barons and defense contractors, I suppose. Still, she has a point. If evil is defined as rampant chaos and destruction, then it seems like Iraq has had more than its share since the U.S. – led invasion of 2003. What is less clear to me is the source of all that evil. I suspect it isn't the design of God so much as it is the nature of man.

We are a fickle people. One minute we're declaring our love for all mankind, and in the next we are suing our neighbors, berating our buddies, bombing our so-called enemies, and stomping the crud out of a wounded man, falsely accusing him of wrongdoing. All in the name of God, country, and the fear that compels us.

Thanks to the Department of Homeland Security and CNN's ticker tape alerts, Americans live in a state of relentless anxiety. Car bombs in Iraq. Children strapped with explosives in Afghanistan. Bombs on the subway in London. Chariots of fire smashing through the Glasgow Airport in Scotland. On and on the headlines roar.

I don't know if the information age has made us all that much wiser, but it sure has escalated our fear factor. Alzheimer's, heart disease, breast cancer, colon cancer, skin cancer. Kidnappers, pedophiles, homosexuals, gangs, drunk drivers, thieves, imposters. Mutilations, beheadings, nuclear threats, torture, terrorists, Hezbollah, al-Qaeda, bin Laden, Hugo Chávez, Kim Jong. And for some, George W. Bush. Tsunami, floods, earthquakes, volcanoes, tornadoes, hurricanes, global warming, Arctic meltdown.

Gone are the days when our biggest worry was making sure our kids were up to date on their immunizations, that their shoes were on the right feet, that their homework was finished, and that their birthday invites got mailed. We're more concerned with AMBER alerts, school shootings, and sexually-transmitted diseases.

Is it any wonder that according to the National Institute of Mental Health, 40 million Americans age eighteen and older suffer from an anxiety disorder? Eighteen percent of our adult population experience post-traumatic stress disorder, general anxiety disorder, obsessive-compulsive disorder, or phobias of various natures. Neurosis has become as American as billowing flags and apple pies.

We're a nation in repose feasting on fear. We're constantly feeding our insatiable panic addiction. We like having the ever-loving-daylights scared out of us. We really like it. And Wall Street — that jittery black heart that keeps our nation wealthy — banks on it.

The number of horror flicks debuting between 2006 and 2007 doubled, so says a report by National Public Radio. Simple economics, explain the experts. Such movies are cheap to make, and most come with a double- or triple-your-money-back guarantee. What used to pass as extremely gruesome — dismemberment, blood baths, grisly murders — is now mid-afternoon fare.

Eighteen to twenty-four-year-old males and an increasing number of females comprise the target audience. David Poland, who edits *Movie City News*, the online industry journal, and a former avid horror flick fan, is worried about this escalating trend.

"I don't think there is any question that it leads to a coarsening of culture," Poland told NPR. "The question is where that ultimately leads in the spiritual lives of the people watching it."[3]

This heebies-jeebies habit isn't limited to those outside the circle of faith. Sales of books concerning biblical prophecy, foretelling an apocalyptic showdown somewhere along the Middle East's Main Street, have exploded since 9/11. The number of nonfiction books about prophecy sold in the first eight weeks after September 11 increased by 71 percent compared to the previous eight weeks, according to a survey of five hundred bookstores by the Evangelical Christian Publishers Association.[4]

Broderick Shepherd, owner of ArmageddonBooks. com, told a reporter for the *Columbia Journalist* that he pays special attention to news from Israel, where the battle between Good and Evil is presumed to unfold one day very soon.

"If things are bad for Israel, business is good," he said. "But if there is peace in the Middle East, I'm in trouble."

The book rack at Shepherd's store offers such titles as *Jerusalem Countdown, Unholy War,* and *Terrorism and Radical Islam.* He said sales spiked following the terrorist attacks of 9/11 and continue to rise. Hear all the angels sing — Cha-Ching! Cha-Ching!

One of the most bizarre examples of the blinding haze of fear in which we now reside surfaced while I was attending a literary event at Amelia Island, Florida, in the fall of 2006.

My friend Janis Owens, author of *The Schooling of Claybird Catts,* invited me to join her and Michael Morris, author of *A Place Called Wiregrass,* to be part of a panel discussion regarding southern characters. The audience was attentive and responsive as the three of us related our stories of growing up deep-fried and cornbread-fed.

After our presentation, I snuck in the back of an adjoining room to hear a novelist detail his plans for writing bestsellers. He writes blockbuster thrillers. The plot line rarely deviates. The good guys are always white and

American, and the bad guys are always brown-skinned Islamics.

His formula for success is simple. "The people shelling out twenty-five dollars for a book don't want to read about poor dirt farmers," he said. "Write about rich people going to exotic places." (That might explain why Flannery O'Connor didn't die an excessively wealthy woman.)

What startled me and caused the little hairs on my arms to stand on end, however, was this fellow's advice regarding creating action scenes. He spoke of assault weapons (the kind Eric Shannon employed) and covert missions and snipers and all those evildoers, them brown-skinned Islamic bad boys, whose only goal is to rid the world of us good-hearted Americans.

I slipped my hand high in the air. "Do you ever worry that you are contributing to the rhetoric of war and needlessly escalating the fears of your audience?"

"Good question," he answered. Then he gave the crowd one of those over-the-shoulder grins that read for everything like *Naïve peace-loving woman. She must be the daughter of a dirt-farmer.*

He knew all about the intent of terrorists because he has friends in high places, chiefly Special Forces, intelligence operatives and the like. In fact, this modern-day doomsayer was invited by the Department of Homeland Security to employ his novelist skills as a consultant to help our policy-makers and emergency personnel *imagine* all the ways in which evildoers are out to get us. His novels might sound made-up, but don't be stupid; the bad guys are out to get us, he said with a brilliant capped-tooth smile.

One of his books was inspired (if that's the word for it) by the Beslan massacre. The plot-line is the very scenario imagined by the frightened Tennessee mother. (Good grief! Maybe the Department of Homeland Security ought to hire a passel of young mothers to help them figure out all the ways in which evildoers can harm us.) Do you suppose the frightened mom with the aching ulcer has one of his books on her nightstand, next to her dog-eared Bible?

According to this novelist-cum-consultant, Islamic law allows for the killing of children, especially if it furthers extremist ends. Moreover, he notes on his website, the Muslim siege at Beslan was pure evil, displaying a depravity beyond what most of us could ever imagine. His words, not mine. Wonder where was he during the lone-man rampage at Virginia Tech? Or the Oklahoma City bombing? Don't be fooled people. Evil isn't exclusive to Islamic extremists. We Americans are pretty dog-gone good at it too. How else do you explain Abu Ghraib or Columbine?

I'm not sure how the scribe for the Department of Homeland Security would explain the malevolence behind all that. He says that he couldn't devise a scene more terrifying than Islamic terrorists taking our public schoolchildren captive.

But I bet he will. If he wants to keep his career going gangbusters, he'll have to.

If you think about it, in essence his job doesn't differ

much from that of the old-time fire-and-brimstone preacher. The trick is to make your audience feel scared and safe all at the same time, like a child dependent upon the protective care of an abusive parent, the way Eric Shannon and Robin Hocker managed their brood.

Just thinking about all the scared Christians in America today makes me break into a sweat all up underneath my arms. The evidence of things not yet seen no longer defines faith, but has become another sign that evildoers worldwide are busily plotting our demise.

Where's our confidence? Our hope? Where is the peace in the midst of the storm? What is our message to a world rotating on fear? Is it possible that in our hyper-vigilance against our enemies, real or perceived, we've taken our eyes off of Jesus, our protector and Redeemer?

These are a few of the questions I've been quietly pondering as wars rumble on, as global warming heats up, as the pursuit of nuclear weaponry explodes, as savagery seeps through the seams of society, as self-proclaimed prophets and Homeland Security gurus chant their dire predictions, and as families falter.

Where's our Jesus? Where's our hope?

It is in those moments that the witness of one gray-haired granny named Shirley Dunham returns to me. Even under threat of gunpoint and her very life, Shirley displayed a faith greater than her deepest fears.

"Where's your Jesus now?" the intruder asked.

"He's right here," Shirley answered.

My heart cries out for faith like that.

FEAR'S Fangs

MY FIRST MEMORY OF SHEER TERROR INVOLVED A MASKED man. I was seven. Our family had relocated from Fort Benning, Georgia, to Oahu's Schofield Barracks. My father, a staff sergeant, took our family out to a Halloween festival held at the base, where we ate popcorn balls and candy apples.

My older brother, Frankie, and I went with Daddy into the "Haunted Tent." This wasn't one of those jungle camp varieties of tarp-on-sticks, but more like the Army tents seen on *M*A*S*H**, with partitioned off "rooms" full of ghosts and ghouls. Worried that our younger sister, Linda, was too little for the scary stuff, Mama hung back with her.

I was sticking pretty close to my father's side. As we rounded a corner, a werewolf pulled down the top of one of the partitions and growled angrily at me. I screamed bloody murder and scurried up my father's leg like a de-ranged squirrel. Strong as he was, my father could not shake me loose. I clawed at his neck and bawled like somebody was beating the ever-loving daylights out of me.

The werewolf yanked off his mask lickety-quick and tried to calm me. "It's okay, honey. See, it isn't real," a grinning soldier said. But the damage was done. I wasn't about to let some fanged critter from the dark beyond come near me. I cried louder. Daddy, if his laughter was any indication, found my overreaction and the soldier's attempt at consolation amusing. "Hush, Karen. It's okay," he said, rubbing his hand down my back.

But I would not be hushed. I kept crying — at the top of my lungs — until finally, Mama came to retrieve me from my father's arms. As I recall, she didn't find the scenario as entertaining as Daddy did. I'm not sure, but I suspect that may have been the moment that earned me the title of the family's hysterical child.

<< >>

My husband's earliest memory of fear happened shortly after his family relocated from Portland, Oregon, to the Chiapas Province of Mexico, where his parents served as missionaries with Wycliffe Bible Translators.

The family headed out to the river one afternoon, and like most boys his age — seven — Tim ran off ahead of everyone else. As soon as he reached the water, he did what boys do — he dove right in, never giving a moment's thought to the fact that he didn't know how to swim. The current was strong, swift. It immediately took Tim under and rushed him downriver. Like a rigged bobber, he'd surface every now and then, but he was quickly pulled farther from shore.

When his parents reached the river bank, Tim was gone. Panicked, they began asking around, had anyone seen their son? One lady pointed downstream. She'd seen him wade out into the river but never dreamed he didn't know how to swim.

Little Timmie was gulping minnows and snorting slime, hoping like heck that somebody would help him soon.

Tim's father rushed to grab a canoe, then headed beyond the shelf of lava rock into the deep waters after his bobbing boy, eventually pulling him to the safety of his mother's waiting arms.

Despite being justly afraid, Tim did not panic. He wasn't screaming, and he denies crying. (His mother corroborates the calm reserve of her firstborn.)

Fear is natural and a good thing, when rightfully heeded. It can prevent us from harming ourselves or others. It serves as a protection, an armor that keeps us out of harm's way, or an alert warning us of very clear and present dangers.

Tim had reason to be scared. He was in deep waters. He was, literally, way over his head in trouble. Had his father not come to his rescue, Tim's life may very well have ended that day.

Unlike me. I was never in any danger, yet, hard as they tried, nobody could convince me otherwise. I was in complete hysteria over an imagined threat. A threat that felt more real to me than Tim's truly terrifying situation did to him.

The problem is that children often can't make the distinction between a perceived threat and a real one. And, increasingly so, fewer adults seem able to either.

Disclaimer: Don't confuse being careful with being paranoid. In 1977, I was working for the Southern Baptist Convention as a summer missionary in Michigan City, Gary, Portage, and various other locales in Indiana. It'd been a busy summer, fraught with activities as I moved from church to church, community to community, working Backyard Bible Clubs and Vacation Bible Schools. I'd survived my first true-life tornado by hiding in a cellar. It was s-c-a-r-y, crouching between the mason jars and jigsaw and praying through the storm.

A few weeks later, Penny, my partner in missions and crime, and I asked the pastor if it would be okay to walk to a nearby mall. We wanted to pick up some souvenirs.

The mall wasn't that far from the parsonage, maybe six blocks, but we had to pass a thicket of trees.

"There's a path to the mall through the trees," Pastor said, "but don't go that way. It's not safe."

So we stuck to the main road, the one that ran directly past the church.

We purchased our trinkets and headed home, making sure we had plenty of time before dark. We got within two blocks of the parsonage when a sedan pulled up in front of us and two men jumped out.

"Stop!" they shouted, opening their suit coats so we

could see their holstered guns. Then they flipped open their wallets, revealing shiny badges, and declared, "Police."

They began to question us. Who were we? Did we have any ID on us? Why were we out walking the streets in broad daylight before God and everybody?

Dumbly unaware that walking in daylight was a criminal offense, I explained that we were summer missionaries with the Southern Baptist Convention and that we didn't have any ID on us, since we were after all, walking, not driving. But that we could easily get our IDs if they would meet us down the street at Pastor's place. They weren't buying it.

"Get in the car," the fellow nearest me ordered.

"Come again?" I said, which is a southerner's way of saying, "I ain't sure I heard you right, redneck."

"Get in the car," he said, opening the rear passenger door.

Now keep in mind that neither one of these fellows had bothered to tell Penny or me *why* the police would want us. Nor did we have any proof, other than their holstered guns and flashing badges, that they were who they claimed to be. They'd pulled up in an unmarked car and after a few minutes, insisted that we climb into the back seat. It all seemed like a poorly developed scene from *Hawaii Five-O*. "Book 'em, Danno."

Penny was a preacher's kid from Atlanta and, needless to say, the compliant sort. She started to get in.

"Don't!" I said.

"Don't what?" She turned toward me.

"Don't get in that car. We don't know who these men are. They might not be police."

"What about the badges and guns?" Penny asked, her jaw gone slack at the very idea of disobeying local authorities.

"This is Indiana," I said. "Anybody can get a gun and badge here."

The po-leece were growing impatient with us. One of 'em slapped open a Wanted poster and put it under my nose.

"You look a lot like these runaways," the fellow said. "And there is a bad guy out there wanting to harm them. We're just trying to protect you."

"You think we are runaways?" I asked. Penny giggled beside me.

"Looks a lot like the two of you."

Penny and I studied the poster, trying to see whatever it was the fellows saw, but the truth is we were a lot prettier than either of those poor displaced girls. Surely that was obvious?

Apparently not.

"Get in the car now," the taller fellow said abruptly.

"I ain't getting in your car," I said. "How do I know you're not the bad guys looking for these two girls? Follow us to Pastor's house or call for a marked car. I'm not getting in your car, not now and not fifty years from now!"

So they called for backup.

Pastor looked totally befuddled when Penny and I came bursting through the front door after having climbed out of a police car with its red flashing lights.

"What's going on?" he bellowed.

"The police think we're runaways," I yelled as we sprinted down the hall in search of our wallets.

"Got to get our IDs," Penny said.

Talk about your police profiling. Just look at what can happen when a girl talks funny and walks like a runaway.

Your mother was right. You ought not get into cars with strangers, especially not fellows who strap guns to their chests. Or explosives of any sort. Robin Hocker would've done well to heed that advice. It would have saved her a prison term and a lot of heartache. Even now, decades later, I still think my decision not to get into an unmarked police car was the right one. I wasn't being paranoid, I was being cautious. Anybody can secure a badge from the local five-and-dime; that does not make them a good neighbor.

But, yes, there have been times when I have let fear have its way with me, only to wake up the next morning without any self-respect. What can I say? Paranoia seduced me. For nearly twenty years, I suffered from aviatophobia. You know what that is, right? Fear of flying. (As I type this, I'm on a belly-flopping flight headed through a Nashville thunderstorm. The flight attendants are strapped in, and someone on the plane has just puked.) Some people are born afraid to fly. Southerners seem particularly susceptible to it. Having grown up in a military household, air travel was part of Daddy's deployments and our family's reassignments, but I don't recall ever being afraid until one fateful summer day. I know exactly where I was the moment it first slew me. It was August 16, 1977. The day Elvis died.

Five days after my brush with the Indiana lawmen (hum it with me, now: *I fought the law, and the law won*), Elvis curled up on a floor in his big Memphis mansion and died, leaving me nothing except a debilitating fear that I had never before experienced.

I've pondered this for many years, especially during those years I would not, could not fly, and I've never been able to decipher exactly what it was about the King's death that sparked such blood-chilling fear in me. Naturally, growing up a southern girl, I thought the order of the world was hinged on God's will and Elvis's hips. I was D-E-V-A-S-T-A-T-E-D when Priscilla up and left him. I didn't blame him one bit for porking up the way he did. His binging was completely understandable. None of us knew anything about his drug problems back then. This was in the day before *People* magazine and TMZ.com, a time when celebrities and politicians enjoyed a public life and a private life.

If Elvis had died in a plane crash, my fear would have some plausible explanation. But he died on a bathroom floor. You'd think I would have developed parcopresis. (I'll let you look that one up for yourself.)

Phobias are by their nature not rational. If reason alone could cure our phobias, we'd do a lot more front-porch sitting and spend a lot less time waiting in line at the pharmacy. Front-porch sitting is important because that's when people are most inclined to let you know when you ain't thinking straight. Down south they'd say things like,

"She's got a case of the simples." Or "She's about as bright as a burned-out bulb." Or, they'd smile and say, very lovingly, "Bless her heart. She ain't right in the head."

It was true. After Elvis died, I wasn't right in the head. My fear of flying might not have been so awful if I hadn't been some 1,200 miles from home and no way to get back except to get on a plane out of Chicago, which I was scheduled to do the very next week. I started praying that very night. For Elvis. For Priscilla. For poor little Lisa Marie. For all the people in Memphis. And for the pilots who'd be flying that big ol' jet airliner due to carry me home.

"Dear God," I cried, "if you get me home safely, I promise to *never ever* get on another plane."

For the first time in my life I understood what "pray without ceasing" meant. I kept envisioning a plane, with me onboard, dropping from the sky like a dirt clod from eagle claws. One quick *poof!* and everything was gone. Dust-to-dust. Ashes-to-ashes.

I didn't have any concerns about what would happen to me after I died. I fully expected Elvis to greet me at the Pearly Gates, singing *Take My Hand, Precious Lord*. It was the getting there that scared the life out of me.

I probably would still be holed up in Indiana somewhere if it weren't for answered prayer. God gave me the grace I needed to get aboard that plane and head on back home. He even sat me next to another young gal, who was headed off to a Christian college in Portland. I took her presence as a sign. She didn't make mention of Elvis's death. Maybe she was from Seattle and more of a Jimi Hendrix fan.

Between 1977 and 1994, I kept my promise — I refused to get aboard a plane. I'd jokingly tell people that I had a bargain with God: As long as I didn't fly, he would make sure I wouldn't die in a plane crash. Not that flying was much of an issue. I was raising four kids. I could barely get to the bathroom without a child underfoot; much less board a plane to Fairhope, Alabama, or some other exotic locale. Even so, sometimes I would wake in the middle of the night, my heart lurching, my stomach wrenched with fear over some nightmare that always involved planes. There was nothing in my life that terrorized me more. I'd rationalize my fear by pretending that it wasn't so much the flying I had a problem with, it was more of a height thing. I'd reason that I'd be perfectly fine flying if planes didn't get more than two feet off the ground. But I wasn't fooling anyone but myself, and even that wasn't working all that well.

In 1993, I began work on my first book. The project required that I travel from my home in Oregon to my hometown in Georgia. I was eager to do the project, but I didn't intend to break a promise to God. I took my oath seriously enough that I didn't want to risk ticking God off.

So I boarded Amtrak and spent four days traveling across scenic America, which isn't nearly so scenic when you're speeding by at ninety miles per hour. By the time the return trip reached Boise, however, I had developed the much-dreaded aforementioned fear of public toilets. I began to bargain with God, again, "Get me off this train, and I promise I will overcome my fear of flying."

He did. And I did.

Tackling the fear that routinely paralyzes a person is no small matter. But shortly after I arrived back in Oregon, I figured it was high time me and God had us one of those front-porch visits. So I sat down in Aunt Grace's wicker rocker — the one I'd hauled all the way from Atlanta atop my Nissan van during a previous trip — and listened as God explained how badly I needed an attitude adjustment.

With bare feet crossed and propped on the porch railing, I pushed back in Grace's rocker and prayed. What I remember most from that prayer was the full realization that there were two ways to approach the rest of my life — in fear or in faith.

I was a washed-in-the-blood-of-the-Lamb believer, but I was not a woman living by faith. I was a person who could spout all the right thoughts about God, but I wasn't in a right relationship with God. I was consumed by all sorts of unspoken fears and a phobia or two. I was like the woman who built a fence in the yard to keep the kids safe, but fearing that the kids might climb that one, built another, then another and then another, until nobody could get in or out the front door for all the fences.

Fear was making my world smaller and smaller. I knew if I let it continue that way, I'd eventually become a prisoner of my own soul. I began praying that very day that God would make me a woman of faith. I asked the Creator to give me the courage to move beyond the borders of my confining imaginations and into the glory of God's imaginings.

I might as well have asked for a Mercedes-Benz. Getting me to give up the fears that I'd cocooned myself in was going to take some undoing.

<< >>

As a young child I lost my father to war. Daddy died in Vietnam's Ia Drang Valley in July 1966. Mama was twenty-nine and had a ninth-grade education. The military death benefit at the time was $10,000, not nearly enough to care for three children — Frankie, twelve; Linda, seven; and me, nine.

Everything about our life changed. As dependents, we could not live on base or attend base schools. The military lifestyle was the only lifestyle we knew, and now it was gone. No more deployments. No need to wait for Daddy to get home for supper or home from the field. Daddy wouldn't be coming home at all. And once Mama returned to work, she was rarely around.

Our family nest had toppled from the tallest tree, leaving us all as frightened as wingless birds. Relentless anxiety became my most constant companion, unwelcome, but ever present. When Mama shipped my brother off to military school, making me the oldest child in the household, my fears reached a fever pitch.

With Mama away most nights, working or clubbing, I devised an escape route from our twelve-by-sixty foot trailer. I would lie on the floor of my bedroom with my head poking out in the hallway. That way if an intruder came in the front door, I'd have time to grab my younger sister and rush out the back door, or vice versa. I would lie awake on that hard linoleum, awaiting the intruder I was convinced was only a few steps away. On the nights Mama was home, I would wait till she fell asleep and then curl up on the floor beside her bed. I felt a safety in my mother's presence that I didn't feel anyplace else.

I think since 9/11 Americans have been living like that — in a nagging state of hyper-alert, twisting our heads every whicha' way, anticipating the intruder lurking down the hall. Is it any wonder we feel so plumb worn out all the time? The spirit of fear haunts our sleep and startles us throughout the day. It causes us to cower in silence and acts as a corrosive salt on our sluggish minds.

Our nation, our world is in desperate need of a safe place to curl up and rest. But in order to do that, we are going to have to figure out who is the greater threat: some imagined intruder? Or the fear we bed down with each night and hang out with each day? How can we separate the imagined threats from the real ones? And even if we are able to distinguish between the two, as people of faith, should our reaction to them differ? Whether we are bobbing in deep water or cowering from a werewolf, shouldn't our response be the same? Shouldn't we be calling out to our Father for help?

Love DERAILED

Several years ago an acquaintance lost her infant daughter during childbirth. Over coffee one afternoon, I had the opportunity to share my faith with her. This bereaved mother studied me cautiously, then, through driving tears, said, "I have to get this salvation thing right, because if I don't, I'll spend eternity without my daughter."

Her sobering response slapped me out of my stupor of spiritual platitudes. This mom, through no fault of her own, would grieve for a lifetime for the daughter she never got to carry home. She was doggone determined that she wouldn't spend an eternity without her baby girl. She followed up her remark with pressing questions about God: Who was he exactly? What did he expect from her? And why should she, or anyone else, trust him?

She wanted more than just the latest media release on

God. She wanted to know God's character. What was his intent toward her? Most important, she wanted to know why would he betray her?

<< >>

Revelation was the first book of the Bible I studied. It was the summer of 1970, hip-huggers, and *God is an Englishman*. I was preparing for my freshman year at high school. Mama bought a blue rug and an orange bedspread — the traditional colors of Columbus High Blue Devils — to decorate my bedroom. I didn't yet know any of the upperclassmen at the school. My brother had attended CHS, but had since transferred to an all-military academy in nearby Alabama. Like most girls that age, I was anxious about my future.

That anxiety reached a fever pitch when I was invited to join a youth Bible study group, sponsored by Grace Baptist Church. I'd been attending the church on my own most of the summer. Though Mama walks with the Lord today, she didn't have much use for God or church after Daddy died. Anybody within earshot the day we learned of Daddy's death knew who Mama blamed.

For two weeks in late summer, the youth of Grace met at a picnic table under sap-scabbed pines at a state park as our youth pastor led us in a chapter-by-chapter study of Revelation. It wasn't long after that study ended that nagging nightmares began.

Insomnia set in. I was plagued by an overpowering sense of imminent doom. I grew scared of my own shadow.

One evening, as red and yellow lights streaked the dark sky outside the trailer house, our family gathered in the dirt yard with our neighbors.

"What is that?" Mama asked, pointing upward at the trail of curious light.

My stomach cinched tight, like somebody had banded it. For a second or two, I was convinced that I was seeing the sky split for the Second Coming of Christ. But I felt nothing of the rejoicing Preacher had talked about. Instead, I was seized by a chilling fear, the kind a Dixie Chick might feel if she were standing on a planked platform, with a noose knotted around her neck and Toby Keith grinning wickedly behind.

Turns out I was wrong. It wasn't the Second Coming splitting the night sky. The morning paper reported that it was some sort of atmospheric gas, the origins of which I've long since forgotten. What I do remember in vivid detail, though, is the terror I felt in that moment standing next to my mother, studying that night sky.

For the rest of that summer and throughout much of the next few years, I was on locust alert. All owing to my own diligent study of the Word:

And out of the smoke locusts came down upon the earth and were given power like that of scorpions of the earth. They were told not to harm the grass of the earth or any plant or tree, but only those people who did not have the seal of God on their foreheads. They were not given power to kill them, but only to torture them for five months. And the agony they suffered was like that of the sting of a scorpion when it strikes a man. During those days men will seek death, but will not find it; they will long to die, but death will elude them.

Revelation 9:3-6

Oh, sure, go ahead and laugh, but terror isn't nearly so funny when you're the one battling it. There's a reason primary kids are taught John 3:16 and "Jesus Loves Me." Generations of Sunday school teachers have understood that such lessons are imperative to building a healthy concept of Creator God.

Having missed out on most of those foundational truths, I was thrust into an unsafe world serving a god crafted after Gene Simmons of KISS. My faith was hardly a source of comfort as much as it was a constant reminder that I had better buck up and do right, or I might be smote by a Heavy Metal Jesus. I'd obsessively check my forehead throughout the day, searching for the seal of God and blackheads.

I'd read through the press kit on God, heard all about him from the pulpit, but I didn't really know him. I knew nothing of his faithfulness. Or of his heart toward me.

I thought of him as simply the busy insect-keeper in the sky, plodding about in a hood and rubbers, waiting for just the right moment to release the latch and rain down locust upon all earthly flesh. I was anticipating the moment when my Creator would betray me.

No doubt, I'd still be cowering under an umbrella on sunny days if I hadn't come face-to-face with the God under the hood. Cautiously, at first, then with more daring, I pressed in, demanding to know, c'mon, God, who are you *really*?

Thankfully, he was nothing like what I had envisioned him to be.

<< >>

Remember those Crayola drawings you made in kindergarten that your mama stuck on the refrigerator door for all to see?

"It's Mama," you'd brag to all your siblings and grandparents. "I drawed it myself."

A grin crossed your grandpa's face while your pathetically untalented and very rude older brother pointed at the hook nose and laughed aloud.

"You made Mama look like the Wicked Witch of the West," your brother said.

"Did not!" you protested. But then, studying upon it again, you realized that you hadn't quite captured your mama's true beauty, but had, indeed, drawn some gruesome caricature of her. So you snatched the picture from the frig, wadded it up, and ran to your room crying. Your mama came in later, sat with you, and said not to worry, she thought it was the most beautiful picture ever, even if it didn't look much like her.

God is like a momma that way. He knows that we often fail to depict him as he really is, but he doesn't take offense or scold us for it. He sits with us and comforts us until we realize what we've done.

Eric Shannon drew God as an angry, scornful judge. I drew God with a scary heavy metal mask. Once, during my reporting days, I met a father who fashioned God into a demented train engineer.

It was winter in Umatilla County. The nodding sun eased into the Pacific Ocean shortly after 4:30 p.m. By the time I walked out of the *East Oregonian* newsroom at five o'clock, the sky was a bruised shadow. I'd called Tim and told him that I wouldn't be home for dinner. I had an evening interview scheduled.

"Remember that teenager who got hit by a train? She's coming home tonight."

The stubble-fields of wheat surrounding Pendleton were sugared with frost. The breath of winter usually brought blinding fog to this stretch of road, but on that night, the air and roadway were clear. I drove in silence, enjoying the stillness. A moment of solitude is hard to find when you're a mom and a reporter.

I had to drive around the block twice before I found the right stucco house. With its arched doorway, tiled roof, and a yard edged by evergreens, it looked like something out of a Grimm's fairy tale. An outside light was turned on, an indication that the home's occupants were expecting someone. I grabbed my notebook, a couple of pens, and trod up the brick walkway. A woman wearing a white blouse and black skirt greeted me.

"He's gone to get her," she said, speaking of her husband and her step-daughter. "C'mon in."

She offered me a cup of hot tea. I took it.

Yellow light from the corner lamp gleamed off the red oak floors. Throw pillows fringed in burgundy and gold sat rigidly against the backs of wooden chairs and in the corners of the couch. A Bible, big as a boot box, sat closed on the coffee table.

We made small talk and waited awkwardly for the homecoming. I collected some of the back-story from the stepmother. She was talkative, in that nervous way of people who feel the need to explain themselves. Five minutes into the conversation and it was clear to me that she wanted me to see things from her perspective. She told me Lila[1] was ten when her parents split up. The divorce had been hard on a girl who had been raised up to believe that, at least in some fashion, salvation was linked to marriage. It was sometime after the divorce, after her father took a new wife, that the girl began to act on her anger, her stepmother explained.

"That's when she started drinking."

The drinking led to sexual encounters. By age fifteen, Lila was pregnant. Because of their faith tradition, abortion wasn't an option. And adoption wasn't encouraged.

Lila gave birth to a baby boy and brought him home to grow up in her father's home. Everyone hoped that motherhood would convince Lila to give up her partying ways, but it didn't.

No one knew for sure if Lila was trying to kill herself the night she walked in front of that oncoming train or if she was so drunk she never heard the frantic whistle. Whatever the case, she wasn't expected to live. The train engineer had seen her there on that track and thrown the brake. Still, the train struck her fiercely enough to send her end-over-end. She lived, but just barely. My editor had warned me that Lila had suffered considerable head trauma. She probably wouldn't be able to answer any questions.

Headlights illuminated the room. Father and daughter were in the driveway. This was Lila's first trip home after eight months of therapy. Would her son, now two, recognize his mother? Would she be able to raise him?

Lila's stepmother stepped outside to greet her. I stayed put, hoping to give the family a moment together.

Fifteen minutes passed, time I spent uttering a prayer of gratitude that to date none of my four teens were exhibiting the sort of self-destructive behavior that Lila had, that I had myself when I was Lila's age.

My husband and I could take little credit for that, for while we'd managed to hold our marriage together, there was many a day when we held on solely because grasping to a fraying covenant was all we knew to do. I was keenly aware that families fall apart because of seemingly insignificant acts of carelessness. The phone call ignored. The supper sitting cold. The missed choir performance. The laundry that piles up in the basement like disagreements neglected. The thank yous never spoken. And a generous helping of blame, spread thick like jam on white bread.

I heard Lila before I saw her.

"I love you, Daddy," she said.

"I love you too, honey," her father answered, easing her wheelchair through the door and guiding her to a spot near the couch. The hard, square lines of the chair cramped the already overstuffed living room. The arched doorways to the kitchen led to a narrow hallway, beyond which were bedrooms, none of which appeared to be handicap-accessible. I wondered if Lila's father would have to carry her into her bedroom if they couldn't wangle her wheelchair down the hall.

Lila's dark chestnut hair was cut short, choppy, as if maybe her own son had snuck into her room one night armed with a pair of safety-scissors and whacked away while his mama slept. It was the result, I knew, of having had her head shaved.

Her skin was the pasty-white of Elmer's glue. Her petite frame drawn to a C, curled down over her core. She could move her arms, but her fingers unwittingly balled into her palms.

"Welcome home, Lila," I said.

She smiled and I saw a hint of the spunky gal she had been, before the alcohol, before the birth of her son changed her from daughter to mother, before her so-called friends cheered on her reckless behavior with high-fives and shouts of "You go, girl!" before the train blindsided her.

Taking out a handkerchief from his back pocket, Lila's father wiped the sweat from his brow. A slight man, with wire-rimmed glasses and graying hair, he possessed a jump-to-it demeanor common to men who've served in the military or who were raised by demanding fathers themselves.

He sat in a straight-back chair pulled up next to his daughter. I sat on the edge of a recliner. Lila's son edged past his mother, past us and into the arms of his grandmother.

"I love you, Daddy," Lila called out.

"I love you too," he answered.

"Is this hard for you?" I asked him.

"Hard?"

"Yeah. To see your daughter this a'way?"

He pushed his glasses back on his nose and smiled broadly. "No. I am so glad to have my sweet little girl back."

"But don't you miss ..." I struggled to find the right question. "Don't you miss who Lila was before all of this?"

"Not at all," he said, reaching over and taking hold of his daughter's curled-up hand. Lila continued chirping, "I love you, Daddy. I love you, Daddy." Over and over again like a hungry parrot waiting for a morsel. Lila's father would intermittently answer, "I love you too, baby."

"I'd been praying for God to send something to stop Lila from her rebelliousness," he said. "I just didn't expect it would be a train."

His answer was delivered with what seemed to me to be an inappropriately cocky smile. The kind a crooked car salesman might indulge moments before he unloads the lot's clunker to some trusting soul.

I shifted in my chair. The fuzzy hairs on the back of my neck prickled like the tips of pine needles. I steadied my pen, took a quick breath, and tried to consider the source of his calm.

"So you think this incident was an answer to prayer?" I asked, forcing a tone of cool detachment to my question.

"Yes," he said, confidently. "It was God's way of stopping Lila."

I tried vainly to swallow the seltzer of protests bubbling up from within. Did this father really believe God had leaned down off the Great Throne of Heaven, and with a swipe of his mighty hand, slapped Lila upside the head, all in an effort to stop her cheatin' heart? Who would serve such a God? And why, why would any parent entrust their child to a Creator with such a sadistic bent? I didn't dare ask. I didn't have to, he was eager to explain.

"Before this, Lila was so rebellious, so full of anger," he said. "I prayed God would give me back my sweet little girl and He has."

Or a Chatty Cathy doll, I thought wryly as Lila called out for the umpteenth time that night, "I love you, Daddy."

"I love you too, baby," he replied.

Later as I drove home, I wept for Lila and the independence she lost the night she walked, headstrong or drunk, or likely both, into the path of a thundering train. She'd struggled mightily but now her fight was gone. All that remained was a shell of the feisty girl she had once been. A girl without a will of her own.

I'd been such a girl. Headstrong. Sassy and ready to defy any who tried to corral me. Like Lila, I was angry. I was one of the lost girls, longing for the companionship of the father slain in war.

I knew Jesus. Knew him personally. As a baby cradled sweetly in fresh hay. As a wizard who walked on water like it was a sea of glass. And as the innocent guy found guilty, stripped and beaten like a slave recaptured.

But so what?

WHERE'S YOUR JESUS NOW?

Any child who has lost a parent, or vice versa, knows that the promise of an eternal hereafter with Jesus doesn't fix the loneliness one feels in the here, the right now.

I don't cop a cocky smile when I tell people my father died in a war so senseless it has marred American history for all generations. It makes me profoundly sad. I miss him yet.

I don't recall the exact words I prayed that night as I drove home from Lila's house, but I remember the overwhelming gratitude I felt because the God I'd come to know has continued to love me through all my ugly, ragged loneliness. Never once has he insisted that I get over it. He never indulged my acting out, but he didn't slap me around for it either.

Even as an angry young girl, I understood that what God wanted from me was not vain, rote devotion. I was willing to walk alongside the wizard Christ who could calm a stormy sea, but not with the bloodied and bruised one. Criminals like him scared me.

Until, over time, I came realize that I'd drawn him all wrong. Given him a hooked nose, pointy teeth, and a sneering grin. I'd made him into the Joker. Someone whose sole intent was to do me harm.

But like a good mama, God kept me company, even in my most fevered state. He offered me comfort and held my hand. He washed me clean when I needed it. And sang me songs, loud boisterous tunes, the kind that drunken firemen sing when they are celebrating just for the sake of celebrating. He told me wondrous stories, funny, delightful tales of people I came to love. Because like me, they were flawed. Their lives were messy. And God didn't go in with a wizard's wand and fix them either. He just loved them. Like he did me.

The best thing of all is that he loves my willful ways. After all, hasn't he made me a girl given to passions and random acts of affection? He loves me like a mama — like a father should.

As I drove past a clapboard house, nearing the turn to Helix, I remember the knowing of that moment. Lila's daddy was wrong. God did not send that train to slam upside his daughter. People make errors in judgment every day. I do it. You do it. Sometimes those errors create minor annoyances, like when we are caught and ticketed for doing 45 in a 35 mph zone. Sometimes, though, those errors can be life-altering, like when we take the corner too fast and veer off the road into a telephone pole, crushing our spine or breaking our neck in the process.

That's not God's way of forcing us to slow down. It is simply the result of our own poor decision-making.

Of course, the more natural inclination is to simply blame God for all that goes wrong in our world. Why didn't he pull the brake? Why didn't he unwrap the cord from my baby's neck? Why didn't he point the howitzer away from the tent? Why didn't he turn the hurricane south?

It's likely Lila blamed herself for her parents' divorce, the way I had for my father's death. If only she had been a better daughter. If only she had helped her mama more. If only she hadn't back-talked her daddy and stressed him out so. If only she had never been born. Maybe if she weren't around, everyone would be happier.

I suspect Lila never understood her value to God because she was raised up in a faith constructed of fear and punishment. Her father believed God mowed her down with a train to teach her a lesson, to put a screeching halt to her willful ways. Could it be that he was more crippled than his daughter?

Was he so afraid that God would never be able to heal Lila's broken heart, that he was delighted to have her spirit severed and her will amputated? That's not faith. That's the mangled mind-set of despair.

The God of Abraham is not some troubled train conductor in search of souls to slaughter. He's the coach, standing along the sidelines, clapping and cheering "Way to go!" when we get it right, and when we stumble, he's grimacing and chiding us to, "THINK about what you are doing!"

The God of all Creation could have crafted a world of people parroting affection to him every five minutes if that's what he wanted, but he didn't. He's a good-hearted lover, who desires only honest adoration. Our brokenness is his brokenness. Our triumphs, his triumphs. He does not strap us to a chair and hold us hostage to his will. But his heart leaps when we choose to sit with him for a while.

Living a life of faith is *not* a no-brainer. Faith requires us to think more critically than we ever have before, because our decisions — the big ones and the little ones — have lasting implications for us, for our children, and for all of humankind.

It is in the knowing God, *really*, that we quit worrying about whether he'll betray us, or turn the locust loose on us. Because it's in that knowing that we understand it isn't about who we are, and what we have or haven't done. It's about who God is, and what he's already done.

Sometimes that knowing comes on the darkest of nights, when all you can really see is the frost-coated stubble of a season passed.

The Religion
of CERTAINOSITY

AS I SIT TYPING THIS, MY PHONE KEEPS RINGING. PEOPLE from all corners of my life are in a tizzy over the troublesome actions of an ailing friend. To be honest, I'm worried too. My friend has cancer. Doctors have handed down the death sentence, predicting that he has a few months to a couple of years, max. The worry is that now that he's home, he might decide to hurry the hand of God.

When I spoke to him this morning, my buddy seemed fine. Said he checked himself out early from the care center where he had been receiving treatment because he had some business to attend to. At the time, his comments seemed mundane. If I had spent two months hospitalized, I'd have some business to tend to as well, but I was unaware of the sort of business he had in mind.

Seems my friend is convinced that someone is trying to kill him. He's suffering from paranoia. Not the mild sort, but the gale-force wind sort, where kindly neighbors become thieving intruders. It is likely that this reaction is a result of his underlying health issues, but the cause doesn't matter. It is now a question of what should we, his family and friends, do about it? So we are talking and praying and seeking wisdom beyond ourselves.

There is an old acronym that defines fear as false evidence appearing real. Paranoia extends far beyond mere fear. A paranoid person cannot be reasoned with. That doesn't make him evil. It only makes him sick. But his sickness may compel him to do horrifying things to himself or others.

That's how we end up with massacres like the ones at Virginia Tech and Columbine.

Thankfully, most of us won't ever suffer from an organic-form of paranoia, but that makes our irrational behavior all that much more troublesome and even harder to defend. Paranoid people aren't the only ones constructing their lives upon false perceptions. We all do it, in small ways and big.

Studies have found that women are more afraid of breast cancer than any other health threat, yet, statistically, cardiovascular disease and lung cancer are greater threats. Only one in twenty-five women will die from breast cancer each year, but one in two women will die from heart disease.[1] So why do we fear breast cancer more?

Because of all the calculated harping by medical and media experts alike. These good people are intent on stopping the ravages of this insidious disease, and apparently, they've been wildly successful in their educational campaigns. That's not to say we should ignore the warning signs of breast cancer. We'd be foolish to do so. But we ought to keep it in proper perspective and take care to not overlook the hard facts regarding our heart and lungs.

We should educate ourselves better so that we are equipped to ask the necessary questions — of our doctors and of our God.

Remember Thomas, the befuddled skeptic? What a bum rap he got after he dared ask some probing questions, like "You saw Jesus? No way! C'mon. What are you smoking? Jesus might have holes in his hands, but you got one in your head. I won't believe it till I see him with my own two eyes."

Listen, I understand why Thomas was so persnickety about all that. I once interviewed a woman who claimed she was a psychic. She also said she'd been having sex with her dead husband. Now I don't want to watch people, living or dead, having sex. By its very nature, intimacy wasn't designed to be a spectator sport. But that interview with the psychic-gal helped me appreciate why Thomas *asked* to see those scars of the risen Lord.

If somebody tells me he's seen dead people risen or that he is having sex with dead people, you'd better bet your bippy I'm going to be asking some tough questions, just like Thomas. That alone doesn't make me a skeptic or rebellious or even lacking in faith, despite what some might suggest.

Many of us who grew up in the Judeo-Christian

tradition were raised up under the mute model of "because I said so." We couldn't ride bikes or iron our trousers on the Sabbath because our fathers said so. We couldn't have a slumber party on Saturday because our mothers said so. We couldn't drink wine, ever, because the Scriptures said so. (When in truth what the Scriptures said was "do not be drunk with wine," but we weren't aware of that fine point then.)

Good Christian women didn't even dare wear trousers because a woman wasn't supposed to wear anything with a fly in the front. I'm sure there was some convoluted explanation for all that nonsense, but I never did ask why. Historically, asking questions of our elders has been associated with being disrespectful or "talking back" or being a "Doubting Thomas."

In recounting the story of Thomas, the gospel author makes a point of noting that Jesus said those who believe without seeing are blessed. But the author left off a disclaimer about the dangers of taking things at face value. Relying on beliefs alone can sometimes make a person dumb as a bovine.

Those wide-eyed creatures have 320-degree panoramic vision, enabling them to see in almost any direction. But that ability isn't worth a lick of beans when it comes to determining a threat. Cattle lack depth-perception. They are frequently frightened by their own shadows. And since cattle are colorblind, their world is full of scary shadows.

There are people like that. People who believe they have the gift of panoramic vision but who lack depth perception. Their entire world is black and white. They see terrifying shadows behind everything. And like their bovine counterparts, they have a tendency to herd up, especially when they feel threatened.

I know all about these people because I used to belong to the herd. I wasn't a bad or ignorant person. I simply thought I had a better view of the world than most outside the herd. We were a special breed of people, tagged and marked members of the religion of Certainosity. We placed a high value on doctrinal creed, foremost in which was the belief that it's better to be right than redeemed.

This is a good time to put your eyes in reverse and reread that last line. Members of the religion of Certainosity would rather be right than redeemed.

Disciples of Certainosity never question anything. They don't think they need to. Thanks to that gift of panoramic vision, they believe nothing escapes them. So these disciples don't have any doubts about themselves, about God, or about the Word of God. They can recite, without pause and in pitch dark, the moment of their salvation. They can also recite all the books of the B-I-B-L-E, or the Qur'an, or the Humanist Manifesto, or whatever rulebook it is they are following. Because if there is anything these folks know for certain, it's their own rulebook, by line and verse.

The religion of Certainosity forbids cross-breeding, but its practitioners come from a wide-range of stock, some well-evolved, others less so. If there was ever a religion designed for all people, then Certainosity is surely it. It is totally indiscriminate, cutting across all borders —

geographic, educational, economic, social, political, gender, race, and age.

It has a wide-base appeal. Baptists and Muslims alike practice it. So do liberals and conservatives. Republicans and Democrats. Homosexuals and heterosexuals. Abortionists and pro-lifers. Pacifists and terrorists.

Salvation is not a prerequisite, though many do claim to have such encounters. At its core, there's really no spiritual component to Certainosity. No mercy and certainly no grace. None is needed because the practice doesn't involve faith or hope, although followers of Certainosity often profess to have had visions.

It's these visions that motivate them to action. Visions inspire them to run for office and invade countries. To strap bombs on their bodies to blow up clinics, schools, and markets. To take to the air waves, condemning all who aren't as certain as them. To burn effigies of their enemies and to declare, in no uncertain terms, war on those who do not embrace their particular ideology.

Law and fear are the compelling forces behind Certainosity. Though adherents claim otherwise. They envision themselves as the bold, brave, daring ones. They do not suffer little children, the elderly, the poor, the disheartened, the disenfranchised, or the disabled. Adversity is simply an opportunity. Cursed are those who can't overcome it.

They consider themselves the "faithful," but it's a misnomer. Faith is the practice of hoping. People of faith struggle with doubt. They readily admit that they don't have all the answers, whereas adherents to Certainosity never question anything. They never give consideration to doubt. They know they are right, and they fail to understand why everyone else can't comprehend the rightness of their ways.

Devotees of Certainosity would rather blow themselves up, and all of us with them, rather than admit that they are afraid or weak or broken. History is replete with leaders who espoused the religion — Hitler, Stalin, Pol Pot, Castro, Osama bin Laden, Dick Cheney — to name a few. These leaders rise to power because they are viewed as being confident and assured, when in truth what they are is simply charismatic and myopic. The doctrine of Certainosity does not make allowances for error. Wisdom and discernment are of little value. Devotees aren't required to reason; they are told what to think and when.

Certainosity may very well be the world's fastest growing religion. Devotees can be found in almost any neighborhood coffee shop or church in America. Sometimes the most well-meaning, good-hearted people are the most ardent followers.

A few years back, I met a young woman at an after-church potluck. This mother of four explained that she'd been having some health problems that had stretched out over the past several months. Her husband was unemployed, so there was no health insurance.

Over a spaghetti dinner, with her infant daughter curled to her breast, she told me the various trips she'd made to the chiropractor in an effort to alleviate the back pain she was experiencing. I told her I'd be praying for her as she was scheduled for more tests that very week.

The results were tragic. She had breast cancer that had spread throughout her body into her spine. Pastor put out a plea for help with the children. My husband and I took in the three oldest children, ages five to ten. Another couple took in the baby. The first week these beautiful children were in our home, they received only one phone call from their father. I thought that was odd but just figured that he was so caught up in his wife's deteriorating condition that he couldn't think past caring for her. I was glad to be of help.

It wasn't an easy task though. I was under deadline for a book, and the children were homeschooled. Their parents were of the persuasion that public schools were nothing more than community dumpsters where humanistic rot was allowed to grow like mold on discarded peanut-butter sandwiches.

I'm married to a public school teacher and hold an education degree myself, so I didn't exactly embrace that notion, but I was familiar with the argument. My own brother and his wife raised six wonderful kids, all home-schooled. And I had homeschooled, albeit reluctantly, my son through his junior high years, per his request.

So homeschooling it was. I worked up lesson plans and insisted upon keeping regular hours, something these kids weren't used to, which surprised me. It was a struggle to get them up and dressed and working by 9:00 a.m. And to keep them working until lunch.

I soon discovered that there had been very little routine to their lives over the previous two years — from about the same time their father lost his job. The children had been shuffled between eleven different church homes, something the pastor knew but failed to mention when Tim and I offered to take in the children.

The church elders also failed to mention that they suspected, or possibly knew that the children's father suffered from anxiety, which may have explained why he had a hard time holding down a job.

Over the next month and a half, the time the children lived with us, I discovered that their grandparents lived in the same town and had wanted to help care for the children, but their father had forbidden it. Seems the grandparents were Catholic, and therefore deemed not to be "real Christians." Fervent about raising his children in the Lord, the father had even burned the Harry Potter books their grandparents had given the children as gifts. He was certain such books posed a threat.

"Because they have witches and demons in them," the daughter explained.

The kids weren't allowed to play T-ball, Little League, or any other sport. Their only interaction with other children was at church. Even their diet was restricted. No fast food. No white sugar. No white flour. No white potatoes — yams, please. These children had never even been inside a McDonald's.

Something I didn't realize until I took them there one night. They poked each other, laughed, then ran into the playroom. From the way they were carrying on, you'd have thought they were at Disneyland. Starring bug-eyed at the slides and colorful balls, the eldest tugged on my arm and asked, "Do we have to pay to play?"

"What?" I asked, not understanding her question.

"Does it cost money? Or can we play?"

"You can play all you want," I replied, my heart cracking. For the next hour, I sat reading a book while they chased each other through plastic tunnels and flopped into the giant ball pen. I could not believe the way Jesus was being used to hem in these children's lives.

Week after precious week was passing. Their mother's health continued to fail. Having lost my own father at a young age, I worried about what the children knew of their mother's declining health. What was being done to prepare them in the event of her death? And what was being done to bring this family together under one roof so that these children could have as many good memories with their mother as possible?

These were the questions I intended to ask when I called our pastor one night after I put the children to bed. His wife answered the phone, and when I asked to speak to Pastor, she informed me that he felt it was best if she addressed my concerns. Oddly, Pastor didn't have any reservations about talking to me when he asked if we would be willing to take in the children. But now that the children were in our home, he felt that this was what, "a woman's problem"?

I'd been a reporter for ten years; ninety percent of my workday involved dealing with men and their problems. But I'd been a Christian long enough to recognize the passive male dominance traditionally perpetrated upon women in the church. The philosophy being that older women are to teach the younger women and that men were to have very little interaction with women because all that talking would inevitably lead to humping. I was only slightly amused by the notion.

I had other things on my mind. Most notably, what should my answer be to the children when they asked about their mother?

"You tell them God is going to heal her," the pastor's wife said rather abruptly.

"Okay," I said. "But what if he doesn't? What if she dies and they have spent the last few weeks of their mother's life in my home? What are we going to tell them then?"

"There is no room for your doubt here. We are claiming her healing," she replied sternly. "You must not give the children any other message than their mother will be healed."

I hung up the phone, went to my room, and wept. I wept for the children, for their mother, for their infant sister. Then I wept for Jesus and for the damage being inflicted on these innocent children in the name of Christ.

To their credit, the elders of the church eventually agreed that there was value to bringing the family together under one roof. They helped secure the family a mobile home and Dad a job. I was on book tour when this young mother died, leaving behind four precious children. I don't know what they were told about why God didn't heal their sweet mama.

I suppose if I were an adherent to the Law of Attraction as put forth in the magical bestseller *The Secret*, there would be all sorts of people to blame for this young mother's death. We could start with her, first, I guess. Health was hers for the taking — if only she'd called it forth from the universe. Or we could blame her husband. If he had practiced the power of positive thinking rightly, he could have flipped through the catalog of the universe and picked out the best health care in the world and had it at his fingertips, along with the gold bricks in the bank to pay for it all.

Or maybe we should blame the doctors who treated her. If only they had known *The Secret*. Rather than trying to cut out the cancer, they could have helped this young mother make a poster board depicting her head on Pamela Anderson's glowing body. This would enable her to see herself as healthy and vibrant instead of sickly and dying. If only she could have realized that the illness was all in her head, and not in her breasts.

But then, maybe it was my fault. My lack of faith. My fear of seeing these children motherless that opened the door for death. But then how could I know any different? I'd never heard of the Law of Attraction. The book wasn't out yet. I didn't know that the universe was just one Cosmic SuperMart, stocked with health and well-being on aisle one, wealth and flat-screen televisions on aisle two, and aisle three dedicated entirely to hardback copies of *The Secret*. If it's the Bible you're looking for, though, you'll have to go to aisle thirty-two at the back of the store.

Sometimes I draw God as a confused old man, shaking his head, rubbing his beard, and cussing under his breath at all the greedy people who've drawn him as the mythological corporate raider Michael Douglas portrayed in *Wall Street.*

God is not a capitalist wizard.

Nor is he a medical magician.

I have read C. S. Lewis, A. W. Tozer, Oswald Chambers, Philip Yancey, Scot McKnight, Beth Moore, Stormie Omartian, Joyce Meyer, and many other literate folks who are a lot smarter than I am about spiritual matters, but I still can't explain to you why God heals some folks and not others.

I've been at the scene of a fifty-two-car pile-up on Oregon's Interstate 84 and witnessed the deaths of young and healthy people, while others, already frail and elderly, some suffering from cancers and other ailments, walked away from cars crumpled like potluck aluminum with only facial abrasions and elbow bruises. I don't know why the good die young and the cranky live forever.

I only know that when I pray, God hears me. My doubts. My fears. My cries for help. My gratitude. My songs of praise. And even the most inaudible, inarticulate of prayers, he hears. And never once has he said to me, there's no room for your doubts. Nor has he ever suggested that I ought to go about claiming stake to anything — health or money or big screen TVs. The gifts he gives are given out of his good pleasure, not because of who we are, what we believe, what we claim. If there is anything I know for sure about God, it's that he doesn't barter in Green Stamps.

Up in SMOKE

In 1998 I made a trip to Nashville during what my cousin referred to as the locust invasion. I might've stayed on I-40 if I'd known in advance the Revelation choir was buzzing through town.

"Happens every seven years," my cousin said, mocking my aversion.

Plague or not, the only things that got left behind were thousands of crunchy husks, created when cicadas, not locusts, got their wings. Translucent wings, with veins shaped in the form of a W, which the old-timers took to be a sign from God of a war to come. (Mm, if only our policy-makers were as good at looking for such warnings.)

At any rate, I was relieved to find out that the shells littering the patio weren't locusts. Revelation doesn't mention cicadas as being a sign of the last times. To be honest, parenting my own four children over the past twenty years has provided enough tribulation to keep me from worrying about plagues of any sort. When my children were all preschoolers, a friend called one afternoon, proclaiming that Jesus surely would return before our kids got to be teenagers. I countered her claim with my own truth.

"There's no way that's going to happen," I said. "Jesus isn't going to let us off the hook that easy. Not after all we put our mamas through. He won't be coming back until we get these kids raised."

Not to make light of the coming tribulations, but I've got a whole new perspective on all these matters. When you've lived with four teenagers, contending with a swarm of ugly bugs doesn't seem like such a big deal. Raising kids made me a praying woman.

My children are all adults now, but some twenty years ago, back before I had chin hair, when I could put my makeup on without the aid of a magnifying mirror, I was in the laundry room separating piles of clothes by color — dark jeans and red shirts in one pile, socks and underwear in the other. Ashley, one of my nine-year-olds, approached me.

"Mom?" she said in a barely audible voice.

"Yes?"

I looked up and saw something I had never seen in my daughter's gray eyes before — fear. A bothersome acquaintance with whom I was too long familiar.

"I need to tell you something," she said.

"What, honey?"

Ashley crossed one ankle over the other, pressed her sweaty palms together, and looked away.

"Remember Saturday when you and Daddy left us girls with Stephan?"

Of course, I remembered. Tim and I had an errand to run. Stephan, our only boy, was twelve; old enough, we figured, to care for his three sisters — twin daughters, Shelby and Ashley, nine, and Konnie, seven. We were gone for less than an hour. Still, it was the first time we'd left the kids without a sitter. We'd both been skittish about leaving our brood.

"Yes?" I said, half-expecting Ashley to tell me Stephan had torn the legs off her Ken doll or he'd knuckle-punched her or her sisters.

Ashley checked over her shoulder to see if anyone else had come into the laundry room. It was clear she was struggling with the moral dilemma of whether she ought to rat out her brother or not.

"Stephan got Dad's rifle and threatened us," she said.

Good thing I was in the laundry room. I needed a change of underwear after Ashley dumped that on me.

"He did what?" I yelled.

Panic-stricken, Ashley talked faster than a telemarketer on speed: "Stephan got into the chocolate chips in the freezer and was eating them. When we caught him, he got Daddy's rifle and said he'd shoot himself if we told you or Daddy. So we promised not to tell, but it scared me."

I reached for my daughter and pulled her close to my chest.

"Oh, honey," I said. "I'm so sorry. I know it scared

you to death. It scares me. Can you hear Mommy's heart racing?"

Ashley nodded.

"Tell me *exactly* what happened. Did Stephan point the gun at you or your sisters?"

"No," Ashley said. "He just threatened to kill himself if we told on him."

I was both relieved and furious. I was inclined to do as Mark Twain suggested — nail Stephan inside a wooden barrel with an air hole, wait a year or two and then plug up the hole.

I didn't even know there was a rifle in the house, much less one within reach of the kids. Had it been loaded? Where were the bullets? Was my son mentally unstable? *Good grief*, he's driving me nuts! I couldn't believe the girls had kept this a secret for several days.

"How come you and Shelby didn't tell me and Daddy right away?" I asked.

Ashley started to cry. "I was scared," she replied. "I didn't want Stephan to get in trouble. I didn't want him to hurt himself."

I didn't bother telling Ashley that what she ought to fear most was that I was about to hang her brother out to dry.

I spent the rest of the afternoon talking with Ashley and her sisters, trying to reassure them that their brother wasn't going to kill himself, that they weren't in trouble for tattle-telling, and that there are situations in life that demand that people speak up, so they were doing the right thing, in spite of the threats their brother made.

When Tim got home, we convened a meeting with our son. At first Stephan denied the story his sisters told us. He insisted they had imagined the entire event.

Our son was not only a chocolate chip thief, he was a bald-faced liar. It's hard to say what angered me more. (Overlooking the seething blame I had toward Tim for not making sure the gun was under lock and key to begin with.) It was clear that we were going to need some professional intervention.

Meanwhile, we implemented two consequences: For the next twenty-four hours, Stephan was allowed to eat only one item — the very chocolate chips that had lured him into his poor decision making. And he was instructed to write a paper on why Do Not Lie was on God's Top Ten list of Thou Shall Nots.

This isn't exactly the kind of warm-fuzzy story a mother wants to share about her family, especially her only son. We got rid of the rifle and took Stephan for counseling. Years passed before we left our kids alone again.

Stephan has grown up into a man of praise-worthy character, and, to my knowledge, the only guns he carries around are replicas from other eras that he employs in living history presentations.

But I often wonder what would've happened if Ashley and her sisters had kept their silence? Would Stephan have continued to use his powers of intimidation over them? How else might he have manipulated them, or us, in his own selfish pursuits?

And what happens to a family or a people or a nation whose daily decisions are motivated by fear?

What happens when we listen to the fearmongering of, say, Pat Robertson? In May 2006, Robertson predicted that the Pacific Northwest (Yoo-hoo, Seattle! Listen up!) was going to get a God-lashing in the form of a powerful storm "as bad as a Tsunami." In January 2007, Robertson appeared on his television show, the *700 Club*, and said God had spoken to him and warned him of "mass killings." He added "The Lord didn't say nuclear. But I do believe it will be something like that."[1]

Took me years to get over the image of Jesus as Gene Simmons, and now I'm not quite sure who I ought to fear the most — Osama bin Laden or Pat Robertson. Call me a skeptic, but I'm leery of people who claim God or Allah has given them a directive that if carried out, will surely put all the rest of us at risk. There was a time when we considered drugging and Velcro-binding people who talked like that. At the very least, we'd lock them up for a day or two, till they got a little more sober minded. Now we give them their own television show and help fund bloated political campaigns.

There's something disconcerting about our fascination with fear. When asked about the violence in his movies *The Passion of the Christ* and *Apocalypto*, director/actor Mel Gibson said that given a choice between a nice quiet bedtime story about lambs or one about the monster troll under the bridge, a child will choose the monster story every time.

I haven't conducted any studies, but I'd venture that

children who grow up in war-torn countries like the Sudan, and now Iraq, might long for stories void of violence. I think Stephen King is a terrific writer, but I don't read his horror books simply because I've experienced enough violence for a lifetime. I don't want or need any more demons invading my imagination.

During my high school years, *In Cold Blood* and *The Exorcist* were two of the books everyone talked about. My high school English teacher assigned *In Cold Blood* for a book report. I read the first couple of chapters then took a zero on the assignment rather than finish the book. When confronted about my decision, I explained to the teacher that I spent a lot of time alone at night, since Mama was a single parent, and that I couldn't read such stuff because it scared the knickers off me. I'll never forget how that teacher totally dismissed my fears with a shrug of the shoulders and a remark about me "burying my head in the sand."

But there is no denying that fear is a stimulus — one that many people enjoy and too many people seek out. Fear raises blood pressure and heart rate. It induces sweating, vomiting, and loose bowels. (Remember that the next time you are tempted to get on a triple-loop rollercoaster.) It can cause dizziness, chest pain, and blackouts. In other words, it's thrilling and oddly addictive.

In any given day, the average American is deluged with fear from all fronts. Fear of Iraq. Syria. North Korea. Fear of cancer, heart failure, and Alzheimer's. Fear of global warming, floods, and drought. Fear of losing income, home, and retirement. Fear of losing spouses, parents, and children. Fear of losing face, money, and personal worth. Fear of homosexuals, Muslims, and Islamics. Fear of flying and dying. I'm sure you've got a long list of your own.

Fear has long been a useful tool for swaying public opinion. Advertisers hype it. Politicians preach it. Dictators and demagogues abuse it. Shoot, parents of all generations have long appreciated the benefit of using superficial or distorted facts as a means of manipulation. "Condoms are only 85 percent effective in preventing pregnancy you know." Or "I've got spies all over this town, buddy. You'd better treat my daughter right."

Hitler used fear as a means of inflaming public sentiment, convincing people that the Jewish financial community had cozied up to the Soviet Union in a conspiracy to sabotage German interests. McCarthy employed the same tool as a means of inciting the American public against free-thinkers, whom he labeled communists.

Through a taut "told-you-so" grin, Pat Robertson warned his viewers, "When lawlessness is abroad on the land, the same thing will happen here that happened in Nazi Germany. Many of those people involved with Adolph Hitler were Satanists. Many of them were homosexuals. Those two things seem to go together."[2]

Military correspondent and author Joseph L. Galloway suggests that calamity fuels Washington's politics:

> Whenever the truth threatens to intrude on the White House pipe dreams, suddenly the Federal Bureau of Investigation seems to uncover another huge

and scary terrorist plot. A dirty bomb to be planted in the heart of an American city. A plot to bring down the Brooklyn Bridge with a blowtorch. Another plot to blow up Chicago's premier skyscraper. A plan for steely eyed killers disguised as pizza delivery boys to attack Fort Dix, N.J., and kill American soldiers.

The latest: A plot to blow up the jet fuel pipeline to John F. Kennedy Airport.

Dangerous enemies are out there, but at the heart of all these journeys into darkness were bumbling fools without money, weapons or even a mastermind. Without everything but an FBI informant keeping them talking for a year or so.

Franklin Delano Roosevelt, in the darkest days of the Depression, declared that the American people had nothing to fear but fear itself. The only thing George W. Bush apparently fears is the absence of fear.[3]

Is it just me, or do you, too, have the sense that ever since 9/11 all sorts of people have been pointing shotguns at us, threatening us into a mute compliance?

<< >>

In 1983 my sister, Linda, was pregnant with her first child. It was an incredibly cold winter in Wallowa county, where Tim and I were living at the time. Temperatures plunged to forty below. The car wouldn't start. The wood stove, our home's only source of heat, devoured logs like a rabid beaver. Snow a foot deep shellacked the mountains and the backyard basketball court.

My kids, all preschoolers then, passed their days playing Care Bears and Transformers. Linda had mentioned that she didn't have any maternity clothes. I couldn't share mine with her since what she lacks in height, she makes up for in boobs, whereas my mammary glands malfunctioned in third grade and never recouped.

I decided I'd do the dreaded thing and sew my sis some clothes. It's not that I don't like sewing — it's that I hate it. The mess of paper patterns and prickly pins, frayed fabric and ripped seams. If I'm sewing I'm ripping seams. Lots of them. Sewing always reminds me of junior high home ec and crabby old Miss Jernigan, who once belittled me in front of the entire class for picking out a print fabric to make an A-line skirt.

"A girl your size ought to get a solid color," Miss Jernigan said.

What did I know? Mama had picked the fabric. I wanted to tell Miss Jernigan to take it up with Mama, but right about the time I started to a girl screamed. She had run her finger up underneath the needle on the sewing machine, and now that needle was poking clean through her forefinger. *Ouch!*

That's one more reason I hate sewing — it's dangerous. A person could put out an eye or lose a finger on those machines.

But for my sis, I'd do anything, including puncture a finger. I love Linda with my whole heart. If she needed maternity clothes, by golly, I would make her some that she'd be proud to wear.

Remembering Miss Jernigan's admonition, I stayed

away from wild prints and bought yardage that wouldn't make Linda look like she was wearing a throw pillow. I chose pale pinks, and one with itsy lavender flowers, a blue calico, and a creamy patterned piece.

One by one, I cut the patterns and spent weeks sewing the dresses. Five total. I worked in the early afternoons, and late into the night, long after everyone else had gone to bed. We were driving up to Linda's home in Washington for Thanksgiving. I wanted to surprise her.

There is a certain amount of pride a person gets when they do something they are loathe to do but give it their heart anyway. I felt that kind of pride after I ironed the last hem and stood back to admire the dresses I'd made from scratch. I couldn't wait to give them to my sister. Linda is always so appreciative for any little thing. I knew that my sacrifice of time and effort would really bless her.

After Tim commented on how nice they all were, I folded them carefully and put them in a brown paper sack atop the dryer so that I wouldn't forget to pack them in the van later.

Then I got to cleaning the house and packing bags for the family. I've never liked coming home from a trip to a dirty house. I sorted all the kids' socks, shoes, jeans, T-shirts, and holiday clothes into piles to pack. I carried a brown paper sack from room-to-room, picking up the waded pieces of discarded drawings the kids had made, emptied wastebaskets from the bathroom and bedrooms into the sack, and when I swept the floors, I put the remains of the dust pan into it too.

Then, as Tim loaded the van, I carried the household

trash to the burn barrel out back. Not long afterward, Tim trudged out through the frozen snow and set the barrel's contents ablaze. He didn't hang around long, no reason to, as cold as it was, and the flames being contained.

It wasn't until later that evening, after the kids were in bed that I went to pack the gift for Linda into the van. The sack was gone. Completely missing.

"Honey, did you see a brown sack on the dryer?" I asked.

"No," Tim replied.

"You sure?" I said, wandering into the mud room, looking on the counters there.

"I'm sure."

I looked in the kitchen, searched the living room, looked in all the bedrooms. No sack.

Then it hit me.

I pulled on my boots and a down jacket and ran to the burn barrel, which was still hot. Grabbing a stick, I began digging around, through the smoldering ashes. I yanked it back. It snagged on something. I lifted it up. There on the tip of the stick was a charred strip of lavender fabric. I recognized it as the hem of one of the dresses.

In my fervor of cleaning house, I had mistakenly picked up the sack from the dryer, thinking it was trash, and carried it to the burn barrel.

All that tedious work, all the labor of love, all that sacrifice gone up in flames. Every stitch, every seam, every dart. Gone, gone, gone. I collapsed there by the burn barrel, in the icy snow, clasped that burnt hem to my chest, looked up at the crystal sky, and wailed like a hurt hound.

My sister would never ever see the work I put into the gifts she would never receive. What a waste. Such a complete waste.

There was no consoling me. I stayed outside weeping until the cold forced me in. Then, I went into my closet and shut the door and cried some more. Tim didn't bother trying to comfort me. He knew there would be no use. He knew how he would feel if it had been him. He let me grieve.

When I told my sis what I had done, she was sweet about it. Never uttered a selfish word or told me how stupid I had been to put the dresses in a paper sack rather than leaving them on the hangers, the way I had started to do.

I felt awful. Even now, twenty some years later, the thought of holding that charred strip of fabric sears my heart.

But it was after my fear focus changed that I understood that if I wasn't careful, life could be like that. I could go about laboring for God, only to get to the end of this journey and look back over the altar of my life and realize all those sacrifices I had made were gone. Burned up in righteous fervor.

If I wasn't very careful, I would be crying over a lot more than dresses burned. Living a life that didn't matter scared me far worse than flying and dying.

JOHN & Jabir

REVEREND FRED PHELPS OF TOPEKA, KANSAS, SAYS HE loves Jesus, but he and his followers at the Westboro Baptist Church spend a great deal of time, energy, and money hating on people. They show up at funerals for American soldiers carrying placards that read "Thank God for Dead Soldiers" or "Thank God for IEDs."

On first glance it looks like these people are antiwar protestors, but that's a ruse they use to get across their real message of hating on homosexuals. Phelps calls them fags. He even has a website for channeling his bigotry: www.godhatesfags.com. I got mixed up with them when a young war widow told me about a group of antiwar protestors turning up at her husband's funeral. I wrote a piece asking activists to be more considerate about where they protest. I urged them not to protest at military funerals, military hospitals, or war memorials. At the time, I didn't know that the bulk of protestors turning up at military funerals were connected to Westboro Baptist.

Everybody was tweaked after that piece appeared in the *New York Times*. The military people were mad at the antiwar protestors. The Westboro Baptist people were mad at the homosexuals. The homosexuals were hating on the fundamentalists. The antiwar protestors, the real ones who showed up at military hospitals and war memorials but not at soldiers' funerals, were hating on me and the *New York Times* editors.

The Reverend Phelps called me. At least I think it was him. Whoever it was never actually said who he was, so it's an assumption on my part, which is a bad thing since it can get a person into a lot of trouble. But I don't know of anyone else who would leave a fifteen-minute rambling message on my voice mail about the wrath of God and fags in America, so I think it was either Phelps or one of his associates.

Phelps claims God has turned his back on America because of this nation's policy of tolerance toward gays. The people at Westboro Baptist don't believe in tolerance. That's a sign of weakness to them. They preach that the funerals for American soldiers are designed to give glory and honor to the military and to make evil human beings (the dead soldiers) equal to Jesus Christ, when all those evil soldiers did was fight for fag rights. (This might be a good time for all of us to start counting to ten, inhaling deeply, and trying to stay calm.)

The people at Westboro claim that the war in Iraq and Afghanistan, Katrina, floods, tornadoes, earthquakes,

IEDs, collapsing mines, even the deaths of the Amish girls gunned down in their own school, are examples of God's punishment toward this evil and hateful nation we call America.

"It is a sin NOT to take pleasure in the wrathful out-pourings of God's justice on this nation," so says a post on their website. "The righteous shall rejoice when he seeth the vengeance: he shall wash his feet in the blood of the wicked" (Ps. 58:10 KJV).

They consider themselves true disciples of Christ, but five minutes of reading through their propaganda is all a person needs to see that what unifies the community of Westboro Baptist is a shared hatred of anything or anyone that challenges their beliefs. Fortunately for the rest of us, truth doesn't rely on belief. If something is true, it doesn't matter if one person believes it or tens of thousands do. And vice versa, ten million people can profess a belief in Winnie the Pooh, but that doesn't mean Winnie is going to be any more inclined to share his honey with them. Winnie can't share his honey because Winnie isn't real.

Belief in something doesn't make it truth.

Just because the folks at Westboro Baptist have decided God is homophobic doesn't make it true.

These aren't Bible-thumpers — they are faith-bangers. People who wear their faith like a distorted limb dangling from a bent spine. Instead of being useful, the unsightly appendage serves only to draw the stares of gawkers and scorn of mockers. People who aren't even aware how bent out of shape their faith has made them. They run around, knocking up next to people and wildly flailing that horrid third limb in anger or disgust.

Faith-bangers are convinced that given the course of this world, there's good reason for us all to be afraid, angry, and guarded. (They call it being alert.) Faith-bangers will point to the latest tragedy as proof of God's wrath upon our wayward world. School shootings? The result of prayer being taken out of school. A federal judge slain in her home? What did you expect would happen when you took the Ten Commandments out of the courthouse? The horror of 9/11? God giving America one more chance to repent or perish. War in Iraq? The start of the Jesus Showdown on Main Street.

Dismissing tragedy as God's corrective discipline has always been an effective way to negate our role in searching for solid solutions to life's travesties. The way Lila's father did when he determined that his daughter's near-death experience was God's discipline rather than the result of Lila's own poor decision making and possibly his.

If we believe that Hurricane Katrina was God's punishment for a modern-day Gomorrah, then we can easily blame the city's sinful inhabitants for the destruction and assuage any guilt we might have about not helping the community rebuild.

This transference of responsibility isn't exclusive to the faith community. After I took a trip to New Orleans in the wake of Katrina, I received a ten-minute lecture from my (former) cardiologist about how stupid people are to live in New Orleans because it is nothing more than a clay bowl waiting for a good flooding. This pious doctor's office is within minutes of the Hanford Nuclear Plant. I wonder what his response would be if a disaster struck his town? Who would he berate and blame then?

Far more frightening than global flooding or death by nuking, and far more dangerous, is this insidious inability of ours to see ourselves in others. Plain old cookie-cutter bigotry is our greatest threat, the one thing most likely to lead to our destruction.

The Reverend Phelps is an equal-opportunity meanie. Most people I know are appalled by him and his followers, who are mostly members of his own family. The Southern Poverty Law Center has identified the church as a hate group. Christians from nearly every denomination, including the most strident fundamentalists, have denounced Westboro Baptist and Phelps. This, of course, only underscores for Phelps the rightness of his theology. He considers anyone who opposes him as evil.

But aren't we just as prone to get entangled in the same sort of wrong-headed behavior?

A poet friend told me the story of when the Westboro folks came to Wyoming on the heels of the well-publicized Matthew Shepard beating death. The poet said the fire crews in town gave the protestors a good dousing. He laughed as he told me this tale.

My buddy Mike Morehouse of Opelika, Alabama, wasn't laughing when he related the events of a memorial service held for one of the town's fallen soldiers. City officials had urged locals to come out to support the fallen soldier's family, and to help shield them from the offensive neon placards crafted by Phelps and his cronies.

Mike said that he was disturbed that many of those who had turned out in support of the fallen soldier's family were acting as ugly and hateful as the Westboro Baptist folks. They resorted to name calling and hurled ugly slurs back and forth.

Or consider how quick people are to lump all Christians into the same flour bin as the Westboro Baptist folks, pointing to Phelps as proof of why all religion is bad. Isn't that like pointing to Stalin as proof of why all government is bad?

I'm tempted to dismiss the Reverend Phelps altogether, except it occurred to me while I was eating a bowl of Frosted Mini-Wheats (chewing my cud, so to speak) that if a person were to tweak Phelps's rhetoric, switching out the word *Muslim* for *fag*, or *terrorist* for *homosexual*, it would sound awfully similar to something Bill O'Reilly or Ann Coulter or any number of strident Republicans or fundamentalist Christians might say.

Pat Robertson has said that Muslims are inspired by demonic powers and that the goal of Islam is world domination.

Notice the similarities between Robertson's rhetoric and Phelps's? Remember when Robertson suggested that knocking off Hugo Chavez, Venezuela's president, would be more cost effective than starting a full-blown war? Or when Robertson said that Israel's Ariel Sharon had been felled with a stroke as part of God's punishment? Doesn't that sound exactly like something Phelps would say?

Like Phelps, Robertson targets homosexuals, abortionists, civil liberties folks, and a host of other people he considers wicked as having stirred up the wrath of God toward this nation. Unlike Phelps, though, Robertson keeps urging people to repent. Phelps says it's too late. America is doomed. The locusts are in a pregame huddle, getting ready to invade us at any moment. Along with all those demonic Muslims, I suppose. How do we sleep at night?

Ambien. Lots of Ambien.

<< >>

My buddy John is an engineer with a genius-level IQ. He makes a six-figure annual income and drives a sports car that he calls the bullet. He's got the speeding tickets to prove it. John works hard. He's a good father to his children and a faithful husband to his wife. The family's entire social life revolves around the church. If you ask John, he will tell you that his faith dictates his life.

John believes that. He really truly believes with his whole heart that his life choices have been determined by his faith in God.

That's why he hates Muslims. They don't believe in the Lord Jesus Christ as their personal Savior. John sincerely believes that there is coming a day when the white-hat Christians will square off against black-turbaned Muslims for the Last Great Showdown on planet Earth. Christians will walk away victorious, blowing the smoke from their guns and singing, *Bang! Bang! I shot you down! Bang! Bang! You hit the ground!*

Until then, John thinks it is our moral and religious obligation to kill every Muslim we can. They are our enemy. He supports the war in Iraq, but he doesn't agree with the way it has been implemented. John says if it were up to him, "I'd nuke 'em all." He didn't say if he'd warn the Christians living in Iraq to get out first or not, or if he'd leave it up to God to get them out.

John thinks tolerance is a bunch of humanistic hooey. When somebody offends him or someone in his family, he prays for the wrath of God to be unleashed on their heads. If you look at him with raised eyebrows and question the lack of compassion behind such a prayer, John will rattle off the Scriptures supporting his rights as a righteous person. I'm very cautious about what I say around John. I take great care to not get on his last sanctified nerve.

He does not return the favor. John has a single-minded fervor of faith that prohibits him from seeing that maybe, just maybe, he's wrong sometimes. Even on the rare occasions when John has been caught doing the illegal thing — like speeding — he never admits that he's wrong. Instead he hires an attorney to fight the ticket on the basis of principle. His principles, which apparently tell him he's got a right to travel at the speed of light.

Right about now you are probably counting to ten again and thinking John is a real jerk. But he's not. If you were to meet him, John might offer to take you salmon fishing or for a ride in his sports car. If you needed $100, John would pull it straight from his back pocket and hand it to you without even asking when he might expect it back. Shoot, John wouldn't even expect you to repay him. He's that kind of guy. Real affable.

Unless, you're an Arab. Even an American Arab. Then John would be highly suspicious of you. If you showed up at his church, John would not invite you home to dinner. And if you worked with him, John probably would be checking over your shoulder to make double-sure you didn't take any extra explosives from the job site. If you were sitting next to John on a plane, he'd be watching you like a hawk, giving you the stink eye. John's a big fellow. So don't try anything. He could take you in a fight.

I couldn't take anybody in a fight, even if I wanted to. So I've never challenged an Arab to duke it out, or anybody else for that matter. But after 9/11, I started acting stupid like my friend John. At airports I would stare at the ladies wearing berkas and think what a good hiding place for bombs and knives that was, up underneath all those folds of dark cloth. If two businessmen got on the plane speaking Arabic, or what I assumed to be Arabic since I don't speak it, I would watch them closely to make sure they weren't acting suspicious. I reassured myself that I wasn't being racist but merely performing my civic obligation.

It's our patriotic duty to be paranoid. A 2006 poll by ABC News and *The Washington Post* revealed that six out of every ten Americans think that Islam promotes violent extremism. Forty-five percent think mainstream Islam teaches intolerance of non-Muslims. And a third believe Islam encourages violence toward nonbelievers. Twenty-seven percent admitted to feeling some prejudice toward Muslims and 25 percent said they harbored racist attitudes toward Arabs. Those numbers were highest among evangelical white Protestants and Republicans.

Not surprisingly that same poll discovered that the more a person knew about Islam the less likely they were to view it negatively. I suspect if that poll were reversed and Islamists were asked about Americans and Christians, the results would be similar.[1]

There's this engineer named Jabir in the same Rotary Club as John. Jabir thinks the only good Christian is a dead one, but he's not as vocal about his beliefs as John. Jabir bows in prayer several times a day, beseeching Allah for the brute strength he needs for the Holy War ahead. That infidel John. He doesn't have a clue what's coming.

They can't see it, but John and Jabir are flip sides of the same coin. The way Pat Robertson is to the Reverend Phelps. John and Jabir aren't real, of course. They are composites drawn from people I know. But Phelps and Robertson are very real, and so is the bigotry they promote.

We may possess expansive peripheral vision, yet if we continually fail to see ourselves in others, we are doomed to live in fear of our own shadows. Always on the run, like a stampeding herd of cattle, startled by the darkness of our own images.

All the Same
but DIFFERENTLY

I NEVER CONSIDERED MYSELF A BIGOT, EVEN THOUGH I despised Asian people, the Vietnamese in particular. Mind you, I didn't personally know anyone who was Vietnamese. It was a bitterness I felt entitled to because these were the people who had robbed me of my father.

Nearly forty years had passed since my father's death and never once, not even after the point of my own redemption, did I feel anything remotely approaching forgiveness for the Vietnamese. Nor did it ever occur to me that they hadn't done anything for which they needed my forgiveness.

I didn't concern myself over the losses the Vietnamese children suffered, or their night terrors. I didn't think about the Vietnamese fathers and mothers or sons and daughters lost. Nor did I worry about how their widows put food on the table. Or how many nights they fell asleep weeping.

I didn't consider the damage done to their neighbor-hoods — the pets killed, the friends scattered, the schools bombed, the teachers jailed, the jobs lost, the playgrounds destroyed, the temples fallen, the books burned, or the limbs shattered. During all of my growing up years and on into adulthood, I focused solely on my pain. Sorrow blinded me. Bitterness warped me.

If anything, I applauded myself for containing my anger and hatred toward my enemy. I didn't wish them harm as some did. I simply dismissed them altogether. If I envisioned them at all, and usually I didn't, it was as a nameless, faceless mass, void of any humanity. I did worse than murder them — I pretended their existence didn't matter to God.

That all began to change after I met Xuan Nguyen at the Fishtrap Writers Gathering (www.fishtrap.org) in 2001 and heard her story. Xuan was fourteen when her family fled the village of Phu Lam after American sol-diers destroyed her home in 1968. Xuan had watched in horror as her five-year-old cousin was killed by incoming mortar. And she tended to the injuries her best friend sustained from the fighting. It was her friend's death that troubled me most. I had some idea what it's like to lose a close friend, though I had lost mine only temporarily to a mental illness. Xuan lost hers for a lifetime.

Tucking her dark hair behind her ear and allowing her tears to flow freely, Xuan stood before a crowded room and shared that she had made an awful decision. She and her girlfriend took refuge underground, waiting through long days for the fighting to cease. Xuan explained that she knew her friend would not live; her injuries were too great. There was so little food, and who knew how long she would be there, waiting to be rescued?

So she ate the little food available and watched helplessly as her childhood girlfriend died. It was a torturous decision, Xuan said, having to choose between feeding a dying friend or possibly starving herself and dying too. A decision no fourteen-year-old should ever have to make, but one forced upon children in the midst of war.

This was just one of the many atrocities Xuan endured as a young girl growing up in a country at war. The warring continued long enough for Xuan to grow into a beautiful young woman, to marry a handsome, brave Vietnamese soldier, and to become a widow and single mother. Even now, many decades later, Xuan continues to suffer nightmares and day terrors from all that the American War in Vietnam took from her.

Xuan was the first Vietnamese to call me friend. She helped me see that we were flip sides of the same coin — women wounded by war, traipsing together across tough terrain. When I went to Vietnam in 2003, I pictured her there. As a child. As a young woman. As a widow. As a native daughter forced to flee her beloved homeland.

It was there, at the base of Dragon Mountain and in a manioc field overlooking the Ia Drang Valley and along the muddy Mekong that I finally recognized my own bloodstained hands. They were clasped tightly around an unforgiving heart.

<< >>

Mental health experts tell us anger is a mask for our fears. We get the most angry when we feel the greatest threat. We are instinctively programmed to fight against that which scares us. Such an instinct enabled us to survive in the jungles when we were threatened by lions, tigers, and bears. Now we employ that instinct in the traffic lanes surrounding Los Angeles and Atlanta, charging ahead to cut off other drivers, cursing at all who get in our path.

We are a loud, angry, revenge-seeking nation. We insist on this notion that God's main obligation is to spank those we mark as misbehavin' and to whup up on those people we don't like much. We don't want God to be our judge, per se, but we sure as heck expect him to be our Avenger.

We distort God into our own personal Terminator. Thus, death by AIDS is the fault of all those wicked reprobates. Katrina becomes God's punishment upon America for supporting the evacuation of Gaza. Woe to anyone who takes away one scoop of soil from the Jewish people! Every tornado, every earthquake, every drought, every genocide, and every hot day is one more reminder that people have got to repent or perish.

No worries for those of us in the community of faith, however. God is our designated hitter, ensuring our personal victory in ball games, in battles, and in finding a good parking space.

Christian high schools win state basketball tournaments because they pray before every game, whereas their opponents are blinded heathens. Soldiers paint bombs with "God bless America" or John 3:16, and say prayers before they blow enemies (i.e., people) to smithereens, all in the name of God-sanctioned capitalistic freedoms. The GOP wins the election because their candidate is anointed by God. The Democrats get religion in hopes that it will ensure them a victory in the next round.

We can find the face of God in watermelons, pizzas, tortillas, tree stumps, chimneys, garage doors, and reflected in pie pans and in New York City skyscrapers. We have this uncanny ability to find God in the oddest of places. Everywhere, it seems, but in the faces of all those people we don't like — our enemies.

Our air waves are charged with "us" against "them" rhetoric. The books that routinely hit the bestseller lists are those whose plot line has a bad-guy terrorist (always someone of Middle-Eastern descent) being pursued by the good-guy American. It's the latest version of the western cowboy kick-ass genre.

I've grown weary of such rhetoric myself. I keep expecting some great Mother Spirit to rise up in protest, shouting "Hush Up! All y'all, get quiet now!" In my mind, this Mother Spirit looks a lot like Maya Angelou. Her very presence commands silence. And when she says "Hush!" even the snakes stop their rattling.

Songwriter/musician Fernando Ortega said societal ruckus was the impetus for his devotional CD *The Shadow of Your Wings.*[1]

"Our culture seems to be getting louder and louder," Ortega said. "It's not only loud, it's in your face. It is growing increasingly more difficult to be in a meditative state."

No question about it. The louder we get, the harder it is to hear from God. But maybe that's the point. Maybe we don't want to hear what God has to say, especially if he's going to show up suggesting that what we ought to do when we are wronged is turn the other cheek, or overcome evil with good, forgive our enemy, or some of that other ridiculous, pious mumbo-jumbo.

But you can bet your last sip of water that as long as we fail to see others the way God sees them, the way he sees us, in tenderness and mercy, evil will prevail, loudly.

<< >>

Two of my grown children are blessed to live in the high desert of Bend, Oregon. For the uninitiated, Bend is God's playground. A place where you can wake up on any given day and take a hike along dazzlingly brilliant waters or silently scale an ancient rock face or roar down the slopes of the incredibly ripped Mt. Bachelor.

Sometimes, if I promise to behave myself, my children will invite me over. If I'm on my best behavior, they'll take me to some special event, like they did on a recent Fourth of July.

We drove out to Coyote Butte, south and east of town, to watch the celebration from afar. My husband Tim and I rode up to the butte in style — sitting on a leather couch in the back of a friend's pickup. That might seem like a redneck thing to do, but it's the type of thing I enjoy. Honest.

Shattered glass stars illuminated the moonless dark as we waited silently, expectantly for the patriotic explosives to begin. Moments after the first of the fireworks erupted, a playful breeze sashayed over the scrub-brush and jagged rocks, carrying with it the obnoxious chatter of a potty-mouthed bigot.

Could somebody please explain to me this fixation Americans have with the f-word? Can you imagine any other word that a person might use to string together uninterrupted dialogue? Here was this manic, drunken woman (she was no lady) yelling so loudly that every being on Coyote Butte could hear her rant:

"Slapping-A! I am so slapping proud to be a slapping American! Yeah! Slapping. I don't give a slap who hears me. I'm slapping happy to be a *white American*! I'm slapping proud to be a slapping white. *Slapping whites rule!*"

I leaned my freckled face up toward that glittered sky and asked my husband, "You think God ever wishes he could tune out the world? Put on an iPod and crank up the tunes? Or stuff some of those foam ear plugs into his ears? Do you think he misses the silence of the earth before us? I bet he misses that kind of quiet. Do you think God ever repents of having made us?"

"I suppose," Tim said. (Did I mention Tim's a man of few words? You think he misses the silence he enjoyed before he married me?)

Sometimes, even on the Fourth of July, I'm embarrassed to be an American. And a lot of the time I feel bad for God. How we must shame him.

Lucky for us, God doesn't play favorites. He loves us all the same but differently, the way a parent loves four children. God doesn't shell out a cup of love for Americans and a fourth of a cup to the Sudanese. God doesn't hate homosexuals or bigots. If you believe the B-I-B-L-E, he doesn't hate anybody. He's not a hateorator. He loved us enough to send his only begotten son to forgive us from all our ignorant, bigoted ways.

I wouldn't do that. Give up my child for a blinkered soul. I'd be more inclined to bury such folks alive, let them pickle in their own bitter vinegar. But I'm not good like God. I don't possess mercy deeper than the wide blue sea. I have a hard time loving people, even the ones I like, much less the ones I don't like.

Yep. It's a proven fact, self-righteousness plagues both the secular and the faith community. Anyone can be a carrier. Cardiologists and rednecks alike.

Fortunately, there's a cure that doesn't require talking to donkeys, encountering ghosts on dark country roads, or having somebody rub spit in your eyes. But it isn't painless. You have to be willing to let God to carve the ugly out.

<< >>

It was a Saturday in late October of 1995. One of those gleaming fall days designed for waxing cars or playing soccer. I'd just finished mopping the kitchen when the phone rang. It was a childhood girlfriend calling to tell me that her brother had tested positive for HIV. Neither one of us were quite sure what such a diagnosis meant, exactly.

What little I knew about AIDS I'd learned from reading about a boy named Ryan White. A hemophiliac and recipient of contaminated blood, the young teen found himself in the unlikely position of having to educate a neurotic nation about the misunderstood illness. Unlike White, however, my girlfriend's brother was not a hemophiliac. Eddy[2] was twenty-five, handsome, and gay.

As the youngest of three children, Eddy was slight of frame and not the least bit athletic, difficult for a child growing up in a community bustling with football players and cheerleaders. Eddy was what we southerners called "a mama's boy." He was also an animated storyteller and a terrific mimic who kept us all in stitches. I loved him dearly.

"What does it mean to be HIV-positive?" I asked.

"I don't really know," my friend replied in a barely audible whisper.

"Is he dying?"

"I don't know, but he is very sick."

"We'll be praying."

"Thank you."

After that phone call, my husband and I began to have late-night chats about homosexuality. Its origins. Its consequences. Its implications for adherents to the religion of Certainosity. Tim and I were roll-call members of the Focus on the Family Group. We listened to Dr. Dobson's broadcasts about the threat of homosexuality and read the alarming accounts in his ministry's newsletters regarding the political agenda of gays. I worried about what would happen if gays took over America. Was it their intent to infiltrate our schools and our churches so they could sodomize our children? Dr. Dobson never suggested such a scenario, but that is where my phobic mind naturally strayed.

Would any of my four children grow up to be gay? And if they did, would they lose their salvation? Would they really face eternal damnation? What about Eddy? I knew he loved Jesus. If he died, would he go to hell? Why was he the way he was? Did God make him that way, or was he a reprobate beyond repair?

If Eddy had been stricken with cancer, I would have called up the church secretary and put him on the prayer chain. I couldn't do that with HIV. So that Thanksgiving, while fat turkeys simmered in deep pans up and down our street, our oven sat cold. Our kitchen dark. Our house silent.

Tim and I told the kids about Eddy, explaining to them as best we could what HIV-positive meant, and about the threat it posed. We did not explain how Eddy contracted the disease. There was no mention then of Eddy being gay.

But we did discuss how we could help his family. I don't recall who made the suggestion, but we decided that the only practical way we could help Eddy as a family was to fast and pray for his health and his well-being.

Someone, maybe one of the kids, said we ought to fast our Thanksgiving meal. We would eat nothing from sun-up to sun-down on Thanksgiving Day. And there would be no making it up later. How could it be a fast if we turned around and ate turkey the next day?

Never before had we fasted as a family. And, never

since, though individually we have. We set a course of action. Individual and family prayer. We each wrote letters to Eddy's sister, to let her know that we really meant it when we said we'd pray for their family. We played games and at sundown, we ended the fast with a dinner of frozen lasagna.

As I write this, Eddy is still hanging in there. His health is greatly compromised and has been ever since he got his diagnosis on that bright October day. He's had a few good years, but he's never been able to return to work or to live without a caretaker. Many of his health problems are side effects to the drugs he takes. His partner took care of him for many years, but when the care became too extensive, a family member with medical training stepped in. Eddy's homosexuality and subsequent HIV diagnosis hurt his family deeply, yet, because they were family, Eddy's siblings never abandoned him.

Instead, they took him into their homes. Gave him shelter. Clothed him. Fed him. Ran him to the doctors and the pharmacy. They carried him to church and to their parents' funerals. All the while they have silently mourned the loss of the brother they once knew, the carefree storyteller who had plans to live the big life.

Because of my deep love for Eddy, I began to question Certainosity. Eddy's experience stirred me to action. I read Jerry and Steve Arterburn's excellent book, *How Will I Tell My Mother? The Story of One Man's Battle with Homosexuality and AIDS*. I wept when I read of Jerry's struggles with his sexuality and even more during Steve's account of his brother's death. After I finished the book, I called their mother and told her how sorry I was about their family's loss.

I lived in rural Oregon, far removed from the awakenings that were occurring in churches and communities in Atlanta, Seattle, Portland, and Denver.

Homosexuality was only spoken about in naughty whispers or heated denouncements. Our pastor rarely referred to the issue, unless reciting the latest dispatch from Focus on the Family. But then the community-at-large, mostly farm families or cowboys, wasn't exactly embracing the notion either.

In 1998 I was nearly run out of town after I wrote a piece about a high school student who was jeered by his fellow classmates as a "faggot." The boy's father, a local lawyer, contacted me and asked me to write about the harassment after his attempts to work it out with the school's administrators failed.

The boy's parents felt the principal had dismissed their concerns over the possibility of escalating violence against their son. Instead, this administrator advised the parents to accept their son's sexuality. Their son was a good-looking fellow, blond, square-shouldered, and cut-jawed. He was an award-winning swimmer and sang in the school's honor choir. Admittedly, he did not fit in with popular "shit-kickers" at school, but he said he was not gay. Not that it mattered to the school's cowboys. To them a gay person was anyone they determined to be a "faggot."

The article posed several problems for me, chiefly because my husband was employed by the same school where the boy was reportedly harassed and because I was considered by many in the community as the spokeswoman for Christian conservatives. What in tarnation would those Christians think of me speaking up on behalf of gays? And what about Tim's job?

There was never any question that I would write the piece, though. Not since that talking monkey turned up in my dreams.

This particular dream began with a yammering monkey, who had an iridescent purple face and butt. (She didn't talk out of that, though, thank God.) I discovered her sitting on a stump in my backyard, jabbing a finger my way and yelling at me to "Listen up!"

"I am listening," I replied, a bit annoyed.

"Beware. A double-edged sword cuts both ways."

"Huh?" I was a little befuddled as to why a monkey knew anything about swords. Was she into fencing?

She repeated her admonishment, urging "heed my words" before scurrying off to the neighbor's yard.

I ran up the back stairs into the house, screaming for Tim. (Not really — this is a dream, remember?) I found him sitting at the dining table reading the newspaper.

"There's a talking monkey in the backyard!"

"Mmmuhh," Tim replied, undisturbed. (Okay, so it's a dream that mimics real life.) "What'd it say?"

"She said I'd better beware of the double-edged sword, and then she gave me a verse."

"What verse?"

"Revelation 1:2."

And that's when I popped up in bed, wide-awake, and

began shaking Tim, who was dreaming at that very moment that he had married that *other* girl. I told him all about the monkey with the purple butt and her warning and the Scripture verse.

"Whadya think it means?"

"Well," Tim said, yawning, "a double-edged sword in Scripture refers to truth."

"What about the verse?"

Tim leaned over and grabbed his frayed Bible and read aloud Revelation 1:2 "[John] who testifies to everything he saw — that is, the word of God and the testimony of Jesus Christ."

"What does it mean?" I wasn't about to ignore the monkey's warning.

"I think it means that as long as you write about all that you see and hear, you're going to piss a lot of people off," Tim said. "Christians and non-Christians."

So far, so good. I've managed to live up to Tim's interpretation of the monkey's warning.

Before writing the commentary, though, I did call the school district and request a closed-door meeting with the superintendent and principal, seeking their side of the story about the harassment. Then I wrote the article.

On the day it appeared in the *Oregonian*, the school principal called an emergency before-school meeting for all the staff. Such meetings are usually reserved for announcing unexpected deaths of students or staff. As they entered the meeting, teachers at the high school were handed a copy of my article. With my husband present, the principal began to discredit the story as rubbish. No such harassment ever took place, he claimed. He failed to mention that I'd given him every opportunity to speak freely and correct the record as reported by the student and his parents.

Meanwhile, back at home, I was getting calls from gay activist groups, seeking permission to run the article in their own newsletters. The thought of gay activists using something authored by a writer known for her conservative Christian views amused me. I declined their requests, unsure of whether I wanted my writing to be used to promote their personal agenda.

<< >>

I didn't know what to make of my own beliefs on homosexuality any longer. All that I had been taught on the subject had come out from societal tradition or Levitical law. I noticed that the same folks who yapped about the perversion of homosexuality still ate lobster and slept with their wives during her monthlies. And I don't know a soul who'd actually stone a child for bad-mouthing his parents, despite what Levitical law has to say about all that.

Even those who cited Romans 1 or 2 Corinthians 12 lost credibility with me, simply because they did not give the same weight of condemnation toward the other sins listed in those verses, sins like gossip, fits of anger, or quarreling. Downright congenial of those gays and lesbians to make their sin so obvious. Helps the rest of us take the guesswork out of who is righteous and who isn't, doesn't it?

<< >>

It's been ten years since I wrote that column. My husband teaches at another school now. On occasion I return to the community where I first worked as a reporter. I was there last week to attend the funeral of a friend's son, a sixteen-year-old killed in a wheat truck accident.

It seemed like the whole town turned out for Cason Terjeson's funeral. My high heels sank in the moist soil as I stood on the slope of a cemetery lawn, listening to Doug Wells and Barb Hodgen conduct the service. At one point, Cason's sister Lydia and several of his friends donned some of Cason's favorite hats. There was the green booney hat he wore during wheat harvest. A Dr. Seuss hat he wore every year on the Cat-in-the-Hat's birthday. (Cason's mama is a librarian.) A Harry Potter hat. A cowboy hat, white, naturally. And an orange and black Oregon State University cap that drew thunderous applause and a few yelps from the crowd. Cason had a hat for nearly every occasion, and as his friends noted, he wasn't afraid to wear them anytime, anywhere.

His family said their bright and articulate son lived by an Eleventh Commandment of his own making: "Be kind to nerds. You may work for one someday."

It's rare to find a kid with the self-assuredness Cason possessed. He was not cocky, but he was confident in the love of his family and friends. Cason wasn't afraid to be different. He wholeheartedly embraced the notion that God and others loved him for who he was, not what he possessed or what he could do. Love like that frees a person.

At the funeral, I caught up with the father of the youth who had been mocked as being gay all those years ago. He told me his son was working to resolve, among other things, the pain he still carries with him from his senior year.

That old adage, "Sticks and stones may break my bones but words can never hurt me" is pure-tee rubbish. A broken bone doesn't take ten years to heal the way a broken spirit can.

I am having a hard time typing this through salty tears as I consider the differences between these two young men. Both came from strong, loving Christian families, but because Cason's friends embraced him for the total nerd that he was, Cason knew a freedom that few of us ever know. Whereas the other youth has been chained to a memory of bigotry that he has, so far, been unable to shake free from.

Listen. I've told you about what happened at that high school ten years ago, but I have refrained from mentioning the boy's name or that of his family. Even all these years later, I'm afraid to. Afraid of the whispers that will surely take place in coffee shops and at backyard barbecues as people familiar with the family discuss, once again, whether the boy really is a homosexual or not. There will be no condemnation of their own bigotry or gossip. The talk will focus on whether the boy is or isn't gay, and how awful for his parents — "Such good people."

I can't for the life of me understand why homosexuality is singled out as the sin of all sins. We accept other sins and the people who commit them as part and parcel of

WHERE'S YOUR **JESUS** NOW?

living in a fallen world. Why are gays demonized by our faith community in ways that those of us who are liars and cheats and gossips and adulterers are not?

Those are the questions I began to ask myself as I dealt with Eddy's illness and the plight of the maligned boy and his family. This seeking was a pivotal time for me, and, ultimately, for our entire family. It was the moment when I began to redefine my faith. The moment when I first admitted to myself, at least, that I could no longer be *so certain* about everything. It was the moment when I began to critically consider what it meant to lead a life of faith in the shadow of doubt.

Like FALLING Snow

DANIEL TAMMET HAS A GIFT. HE KNOWS MORE THAN TEN languages and is capable of reciting 22,514 digits of pi. Tammet is a highly functioning autistic savant. He sees pi as scenery. A very beautiful landscape that looks something like a mountainous river valley that Tammet will actually sketch out for others to see.[1]

Prime numbers give Tammet a pleasant head rush, but he imagines the number six as being hallowed and depressing. He even sees people as numbers. David Letterman reminds Tammet of the number 117 because he is tall and lanky. Tammet also sees days and words in color. Wednesdays are blue, as are all words that begin with W. Tammet explains all this and more in his book, *Born on a Blue Day*.

Tammet says he grew up feeling anxious because so little was known about Asperger's syndrome, the name for his particular condition. He felt isolated, different from his peers, apart from the world.

I'm a writer. I don't see numbers in anything, not even my checkbook, which ought to have numbers in it, but instead has words like *Help me, Jesus!* scribbled in the space where deposits are supposed to be recorded. The only figures I could ever conceptualize visually are number one or number two, as in, did you go number one or number two? For some reason that no one has ever explained to me, mothers are supposed to keep track of this.

Tammet says there are times at night when he's falling asleep that numbers begin to swirl in a burst of white light. Hundreds and thousands of numbers swimming like minnows feeding. Tammet swears he finds this experience beautiful and soothing. Not me. Just writing about it gives me a migraine.

A person doesn't need to suffer from autism to know the anxiety of being isolated. I've felt like the number six ever since I decided that maybe homosexuals weren't responsible for turning evil loose in America. I have family members praying for me. They think I'm one of those flaming liberal journalists who freak dances with the dark side. But the flaming liberal journalists won't claim me either. They think of me as the color red, a real Jesus freak.

If I were a singer, I'd write a song titled "Shunned in the Name of Love." I'd go on tour with a backup group of gays wearing low-cut Wranglers and a lesbian drummer wearing a mustard-seed necklace. I don't know what I'd wear, but I'm sure my gay friends would figure something out and I'd look as hot as Demi Moore.

We'd call ourselves 333 because Tammet sees that as a beautiful number. Or maybe eighty-nine because he says that's like falling snow, and everyone thinks falling snow is beautiful, even me, and I don't like winter. Most people think of hate as a hot word. Not me. I think of it as the coldest of all words. If I saw words in color, hate would be blue. Death blue.

Our song would be a huge hit because nearly every gay person in America has been shunned in the name of love at one time or another. Usually it's by a Christian mother or father refusing to have anything else to do with their gay son or daughter, or vice versa. Christians and homosexuals have been hating on each other for a long, long time.

Most Christians will never admit to this though. They know hating somebody is a sin, so they say things like, "I have a friend who is gay. I don't hate him, but I hate his sin." They never talk that way about other people and their sins. I've never heard a Christian say, "My sister is a slut. I love her, but I hate her sin."

Church folks don't call each other sluts because it isn't Christlike to call people ugly names. When Jesus met a slut, he invited her to play a game of hangman in the dirt and dared the crowd gathered around to throw the first stone. Since Jesus was with the woman, nobody even tossed a pebble her way. But if he hadn't been there, I'm sure that tawdry woman would've been gang-stoned within minutes.

I was talking to this fellow from Washington State University. Ray's real bright, and he looks like Matthew Fox, who stars in that television show *Lost*. Very handsome. I've known Ray for a long time, so I know he loves Jesus a whole bunch. He's what you'd call a committed Christian. The sort of son Christian mothers hope and pray their daughters marry. Ray has given a lot of thought to this problem of homosexuality because he has a cousin who is gay. He loves his cousin and wants God's best for him, but Ray is certain that homosexuality isn't part of God's plan for his cousin. He thinks homosexuality is a choice. Ray thinks his cousin can choose to do the right thing, the God thing, and be a heterosexual.

Ray might be right. I'm sure there are some people, who out of sheer boredom or daring rebellion, decide to flip their toast for a while, just to give it a shot. I met this gal, Kate, at a hotel in Salt Lake City who swore up and down on her mama's Book of Mormon that she wasn't lesbian, but she claimed to have indulged in the lifestyle for a while. Kate claimed she'd even been elected Miss Gay Utah, and heralded in a parade through downtown, wearing her tiara.

Kate's reign caused a ruckus because she was a she and not a he, and Miss Gay Utah was designed for men dressed as drag queens — although, she noted, the official rules didn't specify that women couldn't compete. The crap really hit the fan after Kate's Mormon mama found a flyer broadcasting her daughter's title. Her mama hauled Kate's butt to Bible study and began intensive prayer therapy. I didn't blame her mama one bit. I'd probably have done the same thing, not because Kate wanted to be a drag queen, but because she was a confused drama queen. Kate shrugged her shoulders and said with a coy smile that she believes everyone has dabbled in homosexuality.

"Seriously, I'm not a lesbian, but I've tried it. Hasn't everybody?" she asked.

I shrugged my shoulders. My way of saying, "Nuh-huh. Not me." My daughter Shelby, twenty-five, was shaking her head furiously from side to side. She wanted everybody to know that she hadn't tried it. Come to think of it, very few of the people I know have had same sex sex, as far as I know. I mean I don't really know for sure, but as far as anyone has owned up to, that's the case.

That's one of the reasons I have a hard time understanding why, if a person really had a choice, he or she would choose to be gay. If, say, we saw sex as food, the way Daniel Tammet sees days as colors, then it seems to me that heterosexual sex would be a hot fudge sundae, whereas same sex sex would be liver and onions. Only a select few people would prefer liver and onions over a hot fudge sundae. Most everybody else would scarf down the ice cream, while giving a shout out of "Ewweee! Yuk!" to the liver folks. My husband would choose the liver and onions but not for the sex, just for the real liver and onions, which he likes a lot but I never, ever cook.

So I suppose for some, like Kate, being gay can be an acquired taste, but for most I think it's the way they are wired. The way some people are wired to like liver and some to like hot fudge. I don't know why they are wired that way. But the problem for Ray and a heck of a lot of other people is that God didn't say eating liver was a sin but he does say that a man's lying with a man as a woman is detestable, which is how I feel about liver and onions. I suppose in a perfect world nobody would worry about all this, but we don't live in a perfect world. We live in a fallen world, and we have to make do as best we can to straighten it all out.

Personally, I don't care what other people eat as long as I get my hot fudge sundae when I want it. But Ray, he thinks gay people are going to ruin America by trying to force everybody into eating liver.

"It's the children I worry about most," Ray said. "If they grow up in homes with these gay parents, they are going to turn out gay."

Honestly. None of our four children like liver and onions better than ice cream, even though they grew up in a house with a father who preferred Vidalias to vanilla. I've never met a child who preferred liver to ice cream, but I've heard this line of reasoning before. When I was a girl growing up in Georgia, my Sunday school teachers used it to explain why nice white girls should never date black boys, even if they were good Christian boys.

"Interracial marriages are hard on children. They don't fit in anywhere. That's why God says not to be unequally yoked."

Generations of children have been taught and continue to be taught a church-ordained form of racism by twisting Paul's instructions to the believers in Corinth to not be unequally yoked with nonbelievers. God didn't ban white women and black men, or black women and white men, from dating or having babies. Bigoted people are responsible for that, though they keep blaming it on Jesus.

I didn't know that as a young girl; I just believed whatever I was told. That's how I got sucked into Certainosity for all those years. I thought that as long as you believed something with your whole heart, mind, body, and soul that made it true. I didn't realize that truth isn't made more true by the number of people who believe in it. It can stand all alone like the number four, which Tammet says is very shy and quiet but sure of itself.

A person can go around claiming that homosexuals are responsible for all of our nation's ills, but that doesn't make it true. It's a big, fat, bold-faced lie that is confusing folks and making them forget the truth of the message of Christ, which is that we are to love God with our whole heart, mind, body, and soul and to love our neighbors as ourselves, even our gay or lesbian neighbors. We have got to stop all this hating on each other. Put those stones down before we end up on that hangman's post. We should all take a deep breath and count to ten.

That's what Daniel Tammet does. When he gets confused or stressed, he closes his eyes and counts. Numbers help calm him. Each one, he says, is special, and no matter what he's doing, numbers are never far from his thoughts. I think Tammet views the world a lot like God does us, as a continuum of color and landscape, form and order. Each one of us is special to God and never far from his thoughts.

Exacting REVENGE
on God

I WAS WALKING THROUGH THE ATLANTA AIRPORT IN EARLY October 2006 on my way to catch a connecting flight when I overheard a CNN news anchor make mention of the shooting rampage in Pennsylvania that took the lives of five Amish schoolgirls and left five others wounded. The news host said the Amish community was modeling forgiveness rarely seen in our culture.[1]

That previous Monday, Charles Carl Roberts IV, a milk truck driver, walked into the one-room West Nickel Mines Amish School shortly after 10:00 a.m. and asked the teacher if she'd seen a tool of his that had gone missing. She hadn't, but she promised to let him know if it turned up. When Roberts returned a few minutes later, the teacher and students could hear him loading a gun. The teacher and her mother took off running in search of a house with a phone so they could call 911.

Roberts ordered the fifteen boys and eleven girls to lie on the floor in the back of the room. He brought in the supplies he'd been hoarding: a stun gun, a 9mm handgun, a 12-gauge shotgun, six hundred rounds of ammunition, some flex-ties, and some lumber. Before barricading the door, he ordered two other women in the classroom to take their children and leave. They did. He then ordered all the boys out. Emma Fisher, nine, managed to slip out with her brother, but two of the Fisher sisters remained behind.

Roberts, by all accounts a devoted father of three — two sons and a daughter — then instructed the remaining girls to line up at the chalkboard. The girls did as they were told. He bound the girls' feet together, one to another. Then, as law enforcement clustered outside, Roberts began shooting. Unable to break through the door, the police crashed through the schoolhouse windows. Meanwhile, Roberts shot all ten girls, some execution style, some repeatedly.

It's been widely reported that the oldest of the girls, Marian Fisher, thirteen, asked Roberts to shoot her first in an effort to save the others. For Marian, faith was not simply an ideology to be observed on the Sabbath but a way of life to be lived every moment, even in the face of a peaceful community's greatest threat.

Roberts was not Amish. He did business with them, transporting the milk produced on their farms, but this killing spree was not aimed directly at the Amish community. It was a revenge act toward God. According to last-minute phone calls Roberts made to his wife, Marie, and several suicide notes he'd left around the house, Roberts was angry over past misdeeds — his and God's. It's been reported that he told his wife that twenty years previously, when he was twelve, he had molested two of his younger cousins. The cousins reportedly had no memory of the molestation, but the guilt of that seems to have gnawed at Roberts.

Roberts also made reference to the couple's baby daughter, who'd died after having been born prematurely. Robert's grief got mixed in with the guilt. His anger festered for some time. The death of their daughter had taken place nearly ten years prior. Some have suggested that Roberts purposely selected ten girls to kill — one for each year he'd lived without his daughter. A perverse punishment designed to wound the heart of God.

What better way to exact revenge on God than to attack a community of believers known far and wide for their faithfulness and pacifism? Was Roberts hoping that his violent outburst would cause even the most devoted among us to curse God? Did he receive some momentary pleasure from intimidating others? Did he feel a surge of power, pressing a gun to the heads of young girls while they cried out to God? Was this his way of mocking God? We'll never know the answers to those questions, because as police crashed through the windows, Roberts turned the gun and killed himself.

At the couple's home nearby, Marie Roberts read the suicide note Roberts left her, detailing the bitterness he harbored over their daughter's death: "I haven't been the same since; it affected me in a way I never felt possible. I am

filled with so much hate, hate toward myself, hate towards
God and unimaginable emptiness. It seems like every time
we do something fun I think about how Elise wasn't here
to share it with us and I go right back to anger."[2]

Any parent who has ever lost a child, or any child who
has ever lost a parent, understands that "unimaginable
emptiness" that Roberts experienced. But most of us find
ways to cope with our grief — we seek out a therapist,
we find friends who'll listen, we read poetry or listen to
music, we exercise, we brood, we shop, we pray, we rant,
we weep, and we weep some more.

Experts assure us that anger is a normal reaction to
grief. It's normal to be angry at the doctors who couldn't
do enough or at the driver who drank too much or at
our life-long rotten luck. It's okay to throw tantrums, like
Sally Fields in *Steel Magnolias,* and scream, "It isn't fair!
It isn't fair!" Deep in our hearts, we know we have a right
to our anger. Life was never supposed to end in death.
Death is our ultimate enemy. The thief in the night. The
destroyer at midday.

Like so many of us have done, Roberts blamed God
for his daughter's death. Why didn't God, who is all-powerful and all-knowing and all-loving, protect her? Or, at
the very least, give Roberts advance warning so that he
could have prevented it?

The mothers and fathers of the ten girls that Roberts
shot, and especially the five that he killed, had every
right to do as Roberts did — to beseech and blame God.
Had one of those Amish fathers responded by storm-
ing the Roberts's home and killing his wife or children,

we would've understood. Overcome by grief, we'd say. I might have done the same thing if I were in his boots.

Yet, the blood staining the aprons of those young daughters was still moist when their mothers and fathers, grandmamas and grandpapas reached out in forgiveness to the dead man's family. An Amish man visited Roberts's family the very evening of the killing spree to assure the family that all was forgiven. The Amish encouraged others to pray for the Widow Roberts and her children. When money — a reported $4.3 million — poured into their community from a sympathetic nation, the Amish set up a fund for the Roberts family. The usually reclusive group invited her to attend the funerals of their young daughters.

A grandfather of one of the young victims instructed a group of young Amish boys to "not think evil of this man." Gertrude Huntington, a scholar on the Amish community, explained, "Their hurt is very great but they don't balance hurt with hate." Or, as another Amish community member put it, "We have to forgive him (Roberts) in order for God to forgive us."[3]

When questioned by an NBC correspondent on how the Amish were able to forgive the gunman, a grandfather of one of the victims said, "Through God we are able."

In the year following the shooting, the Amish community at Nickel Mines released a statement reiterating their commitment to forgive, but noting that such a commitment isn't easy: "Forgiveness is a journey ... You need help from your community of faith and from God [and sometimes from counselors], to make and hold on to a decision not to become a hostage to hostility ... Hostility destroys the community."[4]

Grace of this magnitude is rarely displayed in our society. Truth be told, we are often leery of people who are so quick to forgive. We suspect them of being weak minded. People without backbone. If forgiveness is extended because of a religious code of ethics, it usually underscores the assumption that religion is nothing but a crutch. A back door out of a difficult situation.

Typically, the sort of piety the Nickel Mines community displayed would be met with a harsh measure of skepticism by a media jaded by years of scandals in the churches and politicians currying favor from the Christian Coalition. Yet the Amish have been able to silence all critics, while we've stood by, silently shaking our heads in utter amazement at the undeniable strength of the merciful Amish. How do they do it?

<< >>

America is not a nation for the meek, but for the mighty, and we are mighty proud of it. It's justice we seek, not forgiveness. How'd the lyrics of that Toby Keith song go? The one he wrote on the heels of 9/11, often referred to as the Angry American song?

> You'll be sorry that you messed with
> The U.S. of A.
> 'Cause we'll put a boot in your ass.
> It's the American way.[5]

I'm not suggesting that we ought to feel warm fuzzies for Charles Roberts or any of the 9/11 terrorists, or that we ought to invite them over for an afternoon barbecue and a cold brew, but the issue of whether we ought to forgive them isn't debatable. The Amish stated that they forgave because that's what Jesus taught us to do.[6]

The biblical imperative on forgiveness is pretty clear cut. We are to forgive others as Christ forgave us. We are to bless those who curse us. Pray for those who persecute us. We are not to seek revenge. If our enemy is hungry, we should give him food. If he is thirsty, we should offer him a drink. This way, the apostle Paul explains, we will be able to overcome evil with good (Rom. 12:21).

Even so, having such a clear directive doesn't make carrying it out any easier. It took me decades to get beyond the hurt and anger of my father's death. I can't imagine trying to forgive a man who strides into a schoolhouse and executes my innocent daughter, or the terrorist who slams a fireball into the office where my daughter is working.

Indeed, many of the Amish have had trouble coping in the aftermath of the school shootings. They've struggled with post-traumatic stress disorder and survivor's guilt and panic attacks, along with a multitude of other health and emotional problems. The victims who lived through the shooting suffer from a wide range of disabilities, including debilitating paralysis. As a result, some in the community have struggled with a crisis of faith.[7] Understandably so — a commitment to forgiveness and faith does not diminish the memory of such terror.

My friends, Hubert and Lillian Champion of Pine

Mountain, Georgia, lost their daughter, Marjorie Champion Salamone, fifty-three, during the 9/11 attack on the Pentagon. She worked as a program analyst for the Army Program Budget.[8]

At the time, Hubert and Lillian's granddaughter, Amanda, was working for an advertising agency in New York City. She was at her desk when the first of the Twin Towers was struck. Amanda called her mother, Marjorie, to say that she was okay. Not long afterward, a friend of Marjorie's watched in horror from the Pentagon parking lot as American Airlines Flight 77 slammed into the complex. The point of impact? Marjorie's office. Hubert and Lillian learned of the attack as they sat watching the *Today Show,* as was their morning routine.

Hubert and Lillian are not the type of people who harbor grudges. They take their faith commitment very seriously. Even so, the terrorists took from them their daughter. Their grief over losing Marjorie is immense. What forgiveness they've been able to muster up has been earned through much prayer and wrangling with God.

"We both feel sorry for the young terrorists who flew the planes into the buildings," Lillian said. "We believe these men were conned into believing that they would go immediately to heaven and have great rewards."

The Champions have made a conscious choice to try to forgive those who took Marjorie's life because they believe that's what God directs them to do.

"We know that we should forgive those that trespass against us so that God will forgive our trespasses," Lillian said.

Neither parent felt that there was any joy or pleasure to be gained from putting Zacharias Moussaoui to death.

"We felt that as long as he was in prison, in confinement for the rest of his life, there was the hope that he might feel some remorse and come to believe in Christ."

As far as Osama bin Laden goes, Lillian said she and Hubert would like to meet him face-to-face to ask him, "What do you feel you accomplished by 9/11?"

Maybe, Lillian said, if they knew the answer to that question, they might be able to forgive even bin Laden. Maybe not. But their faith compels them to at least consider the possibility of forgiveness for the man who turned their world upside down and inside out.

Lillian and Hubert understand that like praying or studying the Word, forgiveness is something we have to discipline ourselves to practice. We aren't likely to wake up one morning and in a moment of pre-coffee haze declare all is forgiven and we are at peace with the world.

Forgiveness may not be an emotion, but anger is. It was his anger at God that Charles Roberts cited as being the reason for his murderous rampage. As his note said, "I am filled with so much hate, hate toward myself, hate towards God and unimaginable emptiness."

Al Qaeda isn't our worst enemy. We are. We face real peril each and every day that we give haven to hatred, bigotry, and unforgiveness. Paul wasn't just whistling Dixie when he warned believers, "Do not be overcome by evil, but overcome evil with good" (Rom. 12:21). The way the Amish community of Nickel Mines is teaching the world to do.

FEAR Transcended

L. GREGORY JONES IS DEAN OF DUKE DIVINITY School IN North Carolina and author of *Embodying Forgiveness: A Theological Analysis.* Jones believes there is a connection between our fears and our willingness to forgive.

"I believe that there is a direct correlation between forgiveness, which enlarges our imagination and our capacity to love, and transcending fears," Jones said. "Forgiveness is crucial to the capacity for love, and as 1 John puts it, 'Perfect love casts out fear.' I also happen to think that 'perfect fear casts out love,' but that's my formulation, rather than the Bible's."[1]

Eric Shannon's daughter lived in perfect fear of the father she desperately wanted to love and to be loved by. I imagine part of the reason she cried out in such terror as she watched the gun battle between her father and the police is because she felt responsible for her father's death. Hadn't she been the one to pray for that very thing? For God to kill her daddy? I hope one day that she will come to know God the way her grandmother Shirley did. I hope she realizes her prayers did not cause her father's death.

Children process grief differently than adults do. Their worlds are more concrete. If they do good things, they are rewarded for it. They get gold stars on the calendar, extra spending money, or maybe an extra half hour on the computer. Whereas, if they hit their sibling, fail to turn in homework on time, or say a curse word, they are punished for it. There are no gold stars, no extra spending money, and they get put on restriction from the television, computer, or cell phone.

Because of the structure of their world, when bad things happen to them, children often process the bad stuff as being the result of their own inappropriate behavior. Once this pattern of relating to the world is established, it becomes very difficult to undo.

My kids can testify that I hold the black belt in guilt and shame. If my children are acting ugly, I expect them to feel duly awful, and I expect them to apologize for their behavior. I embrace the notion that fear of disappointing me or their father ought to compel them to make better decisions for their own lives. And now that our children are all grown, I urge them to be sensitive to God's leading on their lives. If guilt or fear of retribution keeps them from gossiping or being hateful or running around like wild banshees, well, good. We'd all be better off if Paris Hilton's mama had served her girls a heaping helping of shame and guilt from time to time. Islamic Holy Rollers use Paris Hilton as cause to hurl hate at Americans.

What I don't believe in, though, is useless guilt based in unforgiveness, whether that's an inability to forgive ourselves or others. How can we tell the difference between good guilt and bad guilt? Bad guilt continues to condemn us long after we've repented, whereas, good guilt will free us from our careless ways.

God never intended that we live under a mushroom cloud of recrimination. I have a friend who loves the Lord very much. But because she is the child of divorced parents, the last thing she ever wanted was to end up divorced. Unfortunately, her husband wasn't as committed to the Lord or to her or to their marriage. He had an affair with one of his wife's girlfriends, who just so happened to be the church organist. It was an awful mess for everyone involved — kids, spouses, church members, pastors, friends.

But because my girlfriend was a pleaser — a person who desperately sought the approval of God and everybody else — she tried oh-so-very-hard to fix everything and to forgive her husband and her friend. She even went so far as to bake a cake for the woman who had betrayed her and *ask her forgiveness* for getting angry over the affair.

I don't think that forgiving others means you have to bake a cake for your husband's mistress. Not unless you make it with a strong laxative or substitute salt for sugar, but then that wouldn't be an act of forgiveness anyway, would it?

Before you can truly forgive others, you have to understand that you are forgiven. You don't have to bake cakes or pies or crème brûlée. God doesn't care if you know how to cook like Paula Deen. He loves you and forgives you even if you cook like an Army private. He loves you when you berate your cheatin' mate. He even loves your cheatin' mate. (Somebody ought to turn that into a country tune.)

The apostle Paul tells us in Romans:

> *There is now no condemnation for those who are in Christ Jesus, because through Christ Jesus the law of the Spirit of life set me free from the law of sin and death. For what the law was powerless to do in that it was weakened by the sinful nature, God did by sending his own Son in the likeness of sinful man to be a sin offering. And so he condemned sin in sinful man, in order that the righteous requirements of the law might be fully met in us, who do not live according to the sinful nature but according to the Spirit.*
>
> *Those who live according to the sinful nature have their minds set on what that nature desires, but those who live in accordance with the Spirit have their minds set on what the Spirit desires. The mind of sinful man is death, but the mind controlled by the Spirit is life and peace.*
>
> Romans 8:1–6

In order for us to really experience the life and peace of the Spirit that Paul talks about, we have to understand on both a mental and emotional level the perfect love of God that John spoke about (see 1 John 4:18). As long as we view God as the Great Punisher, we will continue to behave like an abused child, in a constant state of fear and condemnation, unable to give or receive a restorative love and constantly trying to fix everybody and everything.

The problem with forgiveness is that too often we feel like we don't deserve it, and we sure as heck know that the people who have wronged us don't. In an interview with BeliefNet following the 9/11 attacks, Desmond Tutu addressed our struggle:

> Forgiveness is not to condone or minimize the awfulness of an atrocity or wrong. It is to recognize its ghastliness but to choose to acknowledge the essential humanity of the perpetrator and to give that perpetrator the possibility of making a new beginning. It is an act of much hope and not despair. It is to hope in the essential goodness of people and to have faith in their potential to change. It is to bet on that possibility. Forgiveness is not opposed to justice, especially if it is not punitive justice but restorative justice, justice that does not seek primarily to punish the perpetrator, to hit out, but looks to heal a breach, to restore a social equilibrium that the atrocity or misdeed has disturbed.[2]

Tutu aptly holds forth the model for forgiveness established for us by a triune God. The point of Christ's death was a restorative justice. He stood in the breach for us before God the Creator. Our misdeeds are not overlooked or dismissed; they are covered in the blood of Christ and forgiven. Understanding the magnitude of the love behind that action is critical to knowing the perfect love that cast out all fear.

Mariane Pearl, wife of Daniel Pearl, the *Wall Street Journal* reporter who was beheaded by a militant Pakistani group, refused to give in to the anger and fear that hounded her after her husband's death. In an interview with *Newsweek*, Mariane explained why:

> "Terrorism," she said, "is a psychological weapon, even though it uses physical means. It stops you from claiming the world as your own. It stops you from relating to other people. It creates fear and hatred. The only way to fight terrorists, as a citizen, is to deny them those emotions. That is the only thing terrorists don't expect. Everything else they expect: retaliation, bombing, attacks. All of that is exactly what they want. Deny them fear, and they lose."[3]

The psalmist David put it a little more bluntly: "Refrain from anger and turn from wrath. Do not fret — it only leads to evil" (Ps. 37:8).

David spent a great deal of his adult life being pursued by big ugly men with back hair, garlic breath, and razor-sharp knives. He was like Dr. Richard Kimble, falsely accused of his wife's murder, who spent 120 episodes of *The Fugitive* fleeing those who sought to harm him, chiefly the police.

David had similar troubles with authorities. King Saul had ordered his henchmen to do away with David because Saul feared he'd be kicked out of the White Palace. Yet rather than cobble together a plan to overthrow Saul,

David went into hiding, intent to wait upon the fulfill-
ment of God's promises. He encouraged others to do the
same when faced with evildoers: "Be still before the Lord
and wait patiently for him; do not fret when men succeed
in their ways, when they carry out their wicked schemes"
(Ps. 37:7).

If I'd been David, I'd probably have told God to let
Saul keep the throne. I haven't had a job yet worth dying
for. I did have a boss like Saul once — someone I considered a friend but who turned on me. He'd say demeaning
things in front of God and everybody, then insist that I
serve him above all others. He'd test me to see how loyal
I was, then berate me like a jealous lover. It was awful.
While it's true he wanted me gone, as far as I know he
never hired any hillbillies to kill me.

It's taken me a while to get over all that. It still smarts
some. There have been days when I've longed for God
to blow a mighty foul wind from a multiplex dairy farm
his way. And a dozen rant sessions where I pointed out
to God that I was a good employee, dedicated and hard
working, that I didn't deserve that sort of treatment from
anyone, by golly. A few times I even tried to take the high
road — to be gracious and move on — but always ended
up stumbling down the incline, cussing my old boss as I
tumbled tail-over-tail. Finally, a girlfriend pointed out to
me that sucking a wound can lead to a serious, perhaps
deadly infection. She said something about unforgiveness
being like drinking poison in hopes that it would kill the
other person. So I quit.

I'm telling you that hateorade is dangerous stuff. You

shouldn't store it up. It'll make you sicker than a rabid dog on a stinking hot day.

<< >>

Several years ago I attended a Fishtrap Writers Conference that focused on the issue of forgiveness and the unforgivable. One of the main speakers was a woman who had been brutally raped and repeatedly stabbed. Her attacker had assumed her dead and left her in a pool of blood. The victim survived against all odds and was able to identify her rapist.

Someone in the audience asked her if she had been able to forgive her attacker. Not surprisingly she said no, that she wasn't even interested in making any effort to forgive him. Later, over dinner, I heard a couple of people discussing her response. The general feeling was that we all understood why she couldn't forgive her attacker. Yet one attendee noted, "It's too bad, for her own sake, that she isn't able to forgive."

At the time, I figured that was an easy observation for someone (a man) who hasn't been raped, stabbed, and left for dead to make. But later that same night I had another one of those whoo-hoo dreams of mine. God's form of IM-ing.

I dreamt I was standing at the altar of St. Joseph Catholic Church in Macon, Georgia. For the record, I am not Catholic, but I had visited this magnificent church once while in town on business. St. Joseph's has over sixty stained-glass windows, most of which were crafted in Bavaria. The gilded columns, which rise eighty feet to support the multi-spired roof, come from Georgia quarries. Standing inside St. Joseph's is like spinning in the center of a colorful kaleidoscope. The dream went like this:

In my hands, I grasped the stem of a golden chalice. Stretched out before me was a line of people, all holding their own golden goblets. Only, mine was empty and theirs were full. As I studied their faces, I realized these were people I knew. Pastor Smitty and his wife Betty. My sister Linda. Mama. My high school English teacher. A music teacher. A youth pastor. Granny Leona. Veterans of various wars that I knew. My girlfriends from high school and college. My husband. Some old boyfriends. Many of my writer friends.

No old bosses, but otherwise, every significant person in my life was there. They approached me one-by-one, pouring the wine from their full cups into my empty one. It wasn't long before my cup was overflowing; wine was running over my hands, down my elbows, all over the floor. And still people kept coming, pouring from their fullness into mine.

"Grace I give to you," each one said as he or she stepped forward.

A river of red wine was running down the aisle of the church by the time I awoke from that dream. The instant message I received was that there are some people whose mugs never get full, some whose cups remain bone-dry their entire lives. These are the cupbearers with soiled clothes and vacant stares. There's a stench to them, a foulness that repels all who dare to approach. These folks are coarse, repulsive. They curse constantly and utter hateful promises of harm and vindication. What they fear most is that others will recognize the emptiness that is their life.

Had it not been for all those people standing in that line, loving me, I'd be one of those scared people with an empty cup. Thankfully, the red stain of grace runs all up and down my arms and puddles around my feet because God deemed me worthy, as he does all of us, and he compelled others to do so, and they did.

The Amish. Desmond Tutu. Lillian and Hubert Champion. They are tapping into the grace and forgiveness that L. Gregory Jones mentioned, the kind of forgiveness that enlarges our imagination and our capacity to love. They are pouring from the grace of their lives into the emptiness of others. And in so doing, they are managing to transcend the bitterness that soaks us all dry.

<< >>

My mama is a wise southern woman with lots of trailer-park smarts. She once told me, "If you don't love yourself, don't expect anyone else to."

When I was thirteen, I had no idea what she meant by that. Now that I'm old as a graveyard dirt clod, I realize that the first person we all have to learn to get along with is ourselves.

Jesus said I ought to love my neighbor, Ethan McDonald, as much as I love myself. Actually, it's not all that hard to love Ethan. He's the football coach who lives across the street. Ethan is what all the high school girls call a "hottie." Mama would say Ethan is easy on the eyes. So is his wife, Sara. She's what all the high school boys call a "babe." I like Ethan and Sara a lot. We go to the same church. They come over and play with our puppy Poe. And I go over there and play with their boy Ryker. Sometimes I'd rather hang with the McDonalds than with myself. They are beautiful people, inside and out. They make life joyous.

It's been a struggle to love myself. Even after I clean up good nobody calls me a babe. My chin has mated with my neck and produced a wee-wobble. I had to give up wearing shorts and bathing suits for national security reasons. Trust me on that. I'm not sure what my real hair color is, or how to best describe my make and model. I have momentary lapses of my brain, bladder, and boobs. The latter are like London Bridge — they all fall down.

I wish I had learned Mama's lesson sooner. I wish I had been kinder to myself. I should've dumped a cup of grace over my head. I should've bathed in the stuff. It took me too long to learn to like myself, and because of that, it took me far too long to start loving others with abandon. I was selfish with my cup. I was afraid God might tire of me and my ways. I didn't understand the nature of grace. That grace is compelled to reach out to those who deserve it least.

Karl Barth said, "Grace is God's good pleasure."

God draws us to him the way Ryker does when he clutches Poe. God holds us close for his own good pleasure. He is not distracted by our wee-wobbles or sagging spirits or our misbehaving. Instead of putting up a fuss, arguing that we don't deserve such affection, and pushing him away, we ought to throw our arms around his neck and say, "Thanks, buddy. I needed that."

But it's hard to understand how Creator God, who knows what we look like nekkid and how we act when our mamas and papas aren't looking, can love us like that. Such love scares us. We keep expecting ol' Gabe to show up tooting his trumpet and delivering a blackmail note, telling us it's time to pay up or be eaten alive by locusts.

The thing is we don't owe nobody nothin'. Not even God. So don't be tricked by some telemarketer with a trumpet.

I didn't have to do a blessed thing to earn God's love. He took pleasure in me not because of who I am, but because of who he is. As the old hymn says, "Oh, how I love Jesus because he first loved me."

In *The Ragamuffin Gospel* author Brennan Manning says, "Self-hatred is an enormous obstacle to loving other people. Usually we dislike others not because we love ourselves too much, but because we're not able to love ourselves enough. We fear and distrust others because we feel inadequate. We hide behind anger, sarcasm or judgmentalism because we're convinced we don't measure up ourselves."

Once we understand God's character and his good intentions toward us, we can quit trying so hard to impress everyone and earn favor. God's good pleasure compels us to love and forgive ourselves first, and then others.

I'm not there yet, but I'm working on it.

A Life of INTENTION

I'M A MIDDLE CHILD WHO HAS GROWN UP TO BE AN AVERAGE person. I don't possess my sister's head-turning good looks or my brother's pencil-sharp intellect. I can't sing. I can't dance. I haven't found the cure for cancer (I never even looked for it), nor have I saved anyone from drowning. I haven't joined a civic organization since I quit Brownies back in 1967. Fact is, I'm anemic in so many ways that I can't even donate a pint of blood to the Red Cross.

I've never helped the lame walk or caused the blind to see. I haven't held a leper's hand or cleaned the sores of an AIDS victim. On my very best day, I've been able to string letters into an e-m-o-t-i-v-e sentence that others on occasion understand. Experts say we writers write because it's our way of claiming immortality — our books will outlast us. Yeah, well so will our silverware, but you won't find me sitting around polishing it all day long.

Still, I've witnessed the remarkable. Moments when I felt God's favor on my undeserving self. Moments of unspeakable joy and quiet grace. Moments of the chilling warmth from moonlight and sunshine.

I can't explain the sacred. I can't explain God. I can't argue the superiority of Christianity or Islam or any other religion. Despite what my husband says, I don't like arguing. A person either believes in Jesus as Lord and Savior or she doesn't, and I do. When I am having a terrible, horrible, no good, very bad day, I repeat out loud that I believe in the cross that Jesus died upon. If need be, I say it ten times, very fast, while holding my tongue. I believe in the cross that Jesus died upon. I believe in the cross that Jesus died upon.... Over and over again, until the message settles the dust devils stirring in my soul.

But my belief alone doesn't make it true. Either Jesus is the Son of God or he's not. Whether three million people believe it or just one person believes it doesn't really matter, because the truth of something is not defined by how many people believe in it or don't. That's the beauty and essence of truth. It is not dependent on us and our limited mental capacities.

During all his years of spiritual seeking, truth was never as important to Eric Shannon as was the power his beliefs afforded him. Eric picked over religions like he was picking through a plate of vegetables, choosing the things that appealed to him most and leaving the others behind. I think a lot of people do that. Sometimes I worry that I've done that.

Gillian Siple, a religion major at a Christian college

in North Carolina, wondered if studying other faith traditions might endanger her own Christian faith. Siple spent a year of study in China, Thailand, and India, where she immersed herself in the religious practices of Muslims, Buddhists, and Hindus. I first heard Siple's story on National Public Radio.[1]

While studying faith practices in Thailand, Siple would wake at 4:00 a.m. to meditate. Meditation is a common discipline among Eastern religions, but some Christian conservatives are leery of it, often referring to it as a tool of Satan. Siple remembered thinking, "What if my friends saw me now? Would anyone recognize me?" She felt so far removed from the person that she had been in North Carolina. Siple said that meditating from 4:00 a.m. to 10:00 p.m. was the most tedious discipline she's ever slugged through.

Still, meditating gave Siple a sense of peace she had not experienced, causing her to worry that maybe she'd gone too far: "Am I still a Christian or am I becoming something else?"

But Siple found when she returned home that her experiences abroad had deepened her Christian faith. She prays, attends fellowships, and heads up an interfaith group on campus, but she also has continued to meditate. What Siple figured out is that meditating has strengthened her faith. The practice made her aware of her every breath, thought, and movement. "The language of intention is as simple as it is profound," she said.

I think what Siple stumbled across in Thailand is a truth. That a person who lives his life with purposed intention is happier and more at peace than a person who swaggers through life without regard. Imagine what life would be like if our every move was one of intention? This truth is the same thing Rick Warren wrote about in his *40 Days of Purpose*. It's what the apostle Paul wrote about when he urged believers to be self-controlled.

Sometimes I worry that being a Christian, believing in the redemption and in the glory of heaven, makes us less inclined to live life with intention. Brad Pitt, who was raised up Southern Baptist, had a crisis of faith that led him to conclude that "I have only one life, here and now, and I'm responsible."[2]

Too often, Christians treat heaven as an escape hatch. No reason to take this life so seriously. We need to quit relying on the hope of heaven as if it were God's hand-written excuse for why we are continually tardy, absent, and unprepared for this life. We might all behave a bit more responsibly if we believed, as Pitt does, that this is it — the only shot we get.

Eric Shannon spent time boning up on various religious ideologies. What he lacked, however, was the discipline to put any of the truth he learned into practice. Many of us lack that mental toughness. That's one of the reasons I've had a difficult time accepting that I'm never far from God's thoughts. There's something about me that always feels inadequate. That I don't measure up. To be fair, there are plenty of times when I have failed. Those disappointments can disturb my sleep and make me restless throughout the day.

I can't figure out why God would be focused on me

when there are so many bigger issues for him to concern himself with — global warming and civil unrest in the Sudan or Iraq for instance.

But what the Scriptures repeatedly tell us is that God is devoted to us. David testifies that he's going to trust in God's "unfailing love." That God's love "endures forever." Colossians tells us that we are "God's chosen people, holy and dearly loved" (3:12).

God cares about all the things we care about and plenty that we don't. I think one of the things I love most about writing is that it gives me insights into God as Creator. Early on I learned a fundamental principle in writing that has served me well: The difference between a good writer and a terrific writer are the details. Was the girl wearing a coat or was she wearing a red coat?

That one principle has helped me better understand how great is our God. He pays attention to the smallest of details. If we were to get lost in a wooded area, God would be able to recall the color of our coats. He's like a mother that way.

Not only does he keep count of us the way Daniel Tammet keeps count of pi, God keeps count of the number of hairs on our head. I think Shirley Dunham knew that about God. She was so sure of his love for her that even with a gun barrel pressing up against her, she was able to testify to God's faithfulness. Instead of raging against her enemy, she took refuge in Jesus.

It isn't that Shirley wasn't afraid. She was. There was no one Shirley feared more than her son Eric. She was aware of the evil he was capable of. Hadn't she warned

Child Services that they didn't know who they were fooling with when it came to Eric? Shirley knew that her son was not a man to be reasoned with, but rather one to be reckoned with.

She knew better than anyone that her son was capable of killing her. In fact, the reason Eric shot her husband Charles, instead of her, was because Eric knew that watching Charles die would be harder on Shirley than her own death. Eric told her, "I ought to kill you, but I think I'll let you live and suffer." Eric's capacity for evil was most terrifying to those who knew him best.

But as frightened as she was of her own son and his damnation ways, Shirley still trusted in Jesus. That doesn't mean that she was counting on Jesus to pop out of that painting like some Comic Scripture Hero and plug a giant finger in the barrel of the gun, then whisking her and Charles through the woodstove chimney to the safety of some hovering protective cloud.

She simply trusted that whatever happened to her — whether she lived or died — God was present. He would never abandon her.

Shirley wasn't sure of Robin's or Eric's intentions toward her, but she was sure of God's. She trusted, wholeheartedly, in the unfailing love of a devoted Savior. Her Redeemer.

<< >>

Trusting God is not as simple as preachers and writers make it out to be, especially when you're carrying around a bruised heart. On the day we learned of my father's death, my mother walked the hallways of our tiny trailer crying out, "Why me, God? Why?" It was a question I prayed over and over again for years to come: "If you're so all-powerful, God, how come you didn't step onto that battlefield and save my daddy?"

I never doubted that God could have reached out and turned that mortar round into granules of steel if that's what he wanted. What I couldn't figure out is why he didn't want to.

When well-meaning people suggested that maybe God needed my father in heaven more than I needed him, I wanted to stomp on their feet, slap them upside the head, and scream: Were you born stupid or did somebody teach you such ignorant ways? Why would a God who has everything need my father more than our family, which was left with so little? Nope. There had to be a better answer than that.

It took years of studying the character of God before I began to understand that death and war are not the handiwork of God, but of man. God is the breath of life. The Scriptures are clear that death is the enemy of God. In his letter to the Corinthians, Paul tells us that the last enemy Christ destroyed was death.

I heard Larry King, an admitted agnostic, interview a family who had faced some tragedy. He asked, "Did you find yourself questioning your faith through all of this?"

Nodding his head the father said, "Of course."

It's a legitimate question. Most of us, when faced with a devastating loss, be it the loss of a child, parent, job, or home, find ourselves asking God, "Why me? Why my family?" But all too often when we fail to get a satisfactory answer, many will renege on the faith that has sustained us in times past.

The thing we ought to acknowledge is that not even God can provide us with a satisfactory answer. There is no answer to justify a little girl being robbed of a lifetime with her adored father. Or to explain away the mindless slaughter taking place in the Sudan. If God himself appeared before us and tried to explain the devastation that was Katrina or the tsunami that struck Indonesia, or even the malady of malaria that's killed millions, what could he say that would make it all okay? How could even the God of the Universe explain the heartbreak of the Holocaust? The torture, the shock, the absolute terror of it all? How should God go about reassuring Eric Shannon's daughter that it was not his intent that she watch officers gun down her daddy?

Ask yourself this — what answer could God give you that would make all the ills of this world okay? What answer would make such devastation all better?

When my daughter Shelby was three, she got her finger smashed by a solid wood door. The tip of her pinky look like hamburger. Shoving her hand into a bucket of ice, I rushed Shelby to the doctor. He sent me seventy miles down the road to the nearest surgery center, where they shaved off the bone and reconstructed her finger.

As they wheeled her into surgery, Shelby held out her arms and screamed for me. The nurse stopped the gurney and allowed me to hold her one more time.

"Mommy's here," I said, crying along with my daughter. "Mommy will be right here."

Shelby relaxed and stopped her screaming. Was she still scared? Sure. Was she still hurting? Yes. Could I repair the damage done? Absolutely not. But what mattered most to my hurting child was that I promised not to leave her. I was going to be there for her.

The problem of *why* will never be satisfactorily answered, but it isn't an issue of God gone berserk. God is specific in his intentions toward us. He came to give us a hope. Hope to see us through our darkest nights. Hope that brings us restoration. Hope that keeps us company when we are lonely. Hope of healing for wounded souls and scarred lands. Hope for a meal to fill our bellies. Hope for a jacket or maybe some love to warm us. Hope that we matter. Hope that we have a purpose. Hope that we can make this a better world for our children's children. Hope for an abundant life now.

It was that sort of hope that Jenn McCollum clung to when her husband, Captain Dan McCollum, was killed in Pakistan in 2002. Jenn was pregnant with the couple's only child. Being a young widow and single mom was not the dream Jenn had envisioned for herself. I met Jenn at a book event in Jacksonville, Florida, after she wrangled her way to the table where I was sitting. She had a handsome blond-haired boy in tow.

"This is Daniel," she said. "He was born after his daddy died."

I stood at that table weeping with Jenn for all that she and Daniel would miss, having missed it myself over the years. Later, during one of our many conversations, Jenn told me that shortly after her husband died, someone asked her, "How can you believe in God at a time like this?"

"How can you not?" she replied.

<< >>

I recently spent a few days in Camp Lejeune with a military widow and her two children. As the daughter of a soldier killed in action, I know a bit about the grief a military family endures.

In February, 2005, a week after returning from his second tour in Iraq, Marine Lt. Col. Richard Wersel Jr., 43, had a fatal heart attack while lifting weights in a base gym. Since that time, his widow, Vivianne, has worked tirelessly on issues related to surviving spouses.

The week I was with her, Vivianne gave a presentation to the troops. This was a mandatory training so the cafeteria-turned-auditorium was packed with service personnel, most all of whom did not want to be there. Vivianne was instructing the troops on the dos and don'ts of being a Casualty Assistance Calls Officer, or CACO, as they are commonly referred to in the military. It is the job of the CACO to tell the family that their son or daughter, husband or wife, has died.

"Nobody volunteers for the duty," one young recruit said soberly. "I can't imagine giving that news to my buddy's family, much less someone I don't even know."

Service personnel are generally assigned the duty. A chaplain usually accompanies them, but it is the responsibility of the CACO to break the news to the family.

The military does not send a CACO out if a person is wounded. They only send a uniformed officer out when that service member has died.

In July of 1966 we were outside our little trailer house tying up a new puppy when the CACO pulled up. Mama said she knew the moment she saw the soldier that Daddy was dead. There wasn't a military base within two hundred miles of that town.

I've heard dozens of stories from widows about the day the CACO came calling. One widow in Texas said she ran out her home's back door and hid in the bushes, figuring that as long as the CACO didn't give her the news, then her husband couldn't be dead.

Another told me that she slammed the door on her CACO and refused to let him in. And one widow in North Carolina thought her CACO had gone through an elaborate scheme to make her think her husband was dead so he could rape her. Your mind does crazy things when you're in shock.

But it was a Marine widow from New York who told me that she taped a sheet of paper over the peephole of her front door so that if a CACO came calling, she wouldn't know it until she swung the door open. She didn't want to know before then.

On the day that Casualty Assistance Calls Officer did arrive, this Marine widow responded to the news of her husband's death with her fists. She lashed out at her CACO with her hands, slapping at him, screaming at him, cursing him.

And you know what that seasoned officer did?

Nothing.

He stood there and took all the abuse that young widow hurled his way. He did not flinch or draw away. He didn't even tell her to stop it.

When's the last time you contemplated walking up to a Marine and slapping him full-throttle across the face? Never?

Well what about cursing one? Have you done that? Or know someone who has lived to tell about it?

Listen. I'm an Army daughter. I can tell you the Marines have no sense of humor. None. Nada. Zippo. They do not take lightly to being called jarheads by folks outside their clan. Much less being cussed at, screamed at, or flailed upon.

But this veteran Marine allowed that young woman her grief.

I think God is like that. He stands before us, offering his mercy for our sorrows, and how do we respond? We strike him. Push him away. Berate him. Curse him. Run from him. Hide from him. Or treat him as a dreaded intruder, blaming him for all that has gone wrong in our lives. We repeatedly fail to realize that the only thing he's come for is to help us if we'll let him.

The military orders the CACO to remain at that family's side for the next thirty days as funeral arrangements and the burial are ironed out. There's a lot of paperwork to be tended to, a lot of decisions to be made, a lot of interference to be run. It is the job of the CACO to juggle all of this, to act as that widow or widower's mediator and go-to person. A really good officer will go beyond the call of duty.

Many will remain involved in that family's life for as long as they are needed — a year or longer. They do the mundane, fetching Happy Meals for the children, helping kids with homework, or running them to baseball games. And they do the hard stuff, fixing the gutters, hanging Christmas lights, mowing lawns on hot days. A good CACO makes it clear to the family that "I'm here for you if you need me, for *anything*. All you have to do is *ask*."

God is like that. Always ready to help. Faithful to go beyond the call of duty. He won't fix all our problems, but he has promised he'll stay at our side, always. All we have to do is ask.

The FRAILTY
of the Faithful

Whenever I head south, my friends Ken and Sherri Callaway welcome me to their beautiful home in Harris County, Georgia. We typically spend our evenings on the back porch, trying to talk over the climatic chorus of cicadas. If it happens to be a warm summer night, a legion of Confederate jasmine shimmies up and over the railing, filling the air with the same sugar-sweet scent found on the toddler who has doused herself with her mama's best perfume. We eat by tea light, starlight, and, if the earth is titled just so, moonlight.

Sherri and I met in the 1970s at the church where I first found safe harbor — Rose Hill Baptist. She was older than me, smarter than me, and prettier than me. She still is, though she probably wants me to point out that she's not that much older. Ken is the grandson of Cason Callaway and Virginia Hand Calloway, whose legacy has been

167

the conservation and preservation of thirteen thousand acres of woodlands in the southernmost region of the Appalachians. Callaway Gardens has served as an educational and recreational resource for families the world over. There are nature trails to hike, biking paths, golfing, water sports, a butterfly center, a vegetable garden, and an educational center, and even a stone chapel.

It was while visiting the Gardens one day that I came across a display of an endangered plant called the persistent trillium. This delicate species has a single whorl of three long, tapered emerald green leaves. Curled directly above that are three itsy-bitsy arrowhead-shaped petals, pure white with pale yellow antlers. The flower turns pink as it ages. And, according to the notes I read that day, it usually grows in forests, on steep slopes or ravines near laurel. About the only place it can be found today is along the Tallulah-Tugaloo River system in northeastern Georgia or adjacent South Carolina. The reason the persistent trillium is endangered is because its habitat has been demolished or fragmented by dams, overgrazing, and clearing.

I have been haunted by that flower. The three white petals and leaves represent all sorts of things to me — the Trinity, the three crosses on a hill, the relationship between a couple and the faith that sustains them. But what has really stayed with me over the years is the flower's frailty.

It grows only in steep places — ravines and gorges — in small clusters of ten or fewer, among a forest of hemlocks and pines. A juvenile will only produce one leaf. The three-flowered blossom won't occur until maturation, about seven to ten years. However, given an undisturbed environment, the plant can live a long life — up to thirty years. That's nearly as old as Grandma Moses.

Suppose we were playing a word association game right now and the card drawn was the word *persistent*. What comes to your mind? Marathoners? Marines? Mother Teresa? Your mother? An old lover, maybe?

I don't know about you, but when I hear the word *persistent*, I think of someone strong, someone willful, someone capable, someone courageous. A person who digs deeper.

I think of my friend Gordon Wofford, who spent nineteen months at Walter Reed Army Medical Center after a sniper's bullet shattered his lower jaw during a gun-battle in Vietnam in 1968. Gordon endured countless surgeries to rebuild his jaw. He had to learn to talk again. To eat again. To find a reason to live again.

I think of Captain David Moses, who fled the Sudan as a fourteen-year-old boy, under threat of his life from the rebels who had killed so many of his boyhood pals. A couple of years passed before he was able to reconnect with his mother and father — assuming him dead, they had held a funeral for him. Eventually David earned a college degree at Weber State University in Utah, where he graduated with honors, and then joined the military, to give back to his adopted country. He's served two tours in Iraq.

I think of my own twenty-nine-year-old mother who had only a ninth grade education when the love of her life, my father, was killed in Vietnam, leaving her with three children and an invalid father to provide for. I think of the thousands of military widows and widowers like her, who have wept over the caskets of dead soldiers throughout history. And the lonely children who cannot be consoled.

I think of Joe Harover, a former neighbor who I first wrote about while working as a reporter for the *East Oregonian*. Joe suffered from Friedreich's ataxia, a progressive neurological disorder. As a boy, Harover had hoped to be a fireman, like his daddy, but the disorder made him clumsy. By his early twenties, while his friends were falling in love and marrying, Joe was clinging to a walker. Unwilling to ask another person to stumble through the dark days ahead, Joe broke up with his girlfriend. When we spoke last, in 2000, Joe was in a wheelchair, weeding among the phlox and daffodils. "If anyone has a right to give up hope, I do," Joe said. He'd contemplated suicide but decided against it after reading Romans 5:2 and 8:1, words that Joe said convinced him of his value to God. "You just gotta keep on going on," he said.

And I think of my friends Ken and Sherri Callaway, who have lost two sons, one at age fourteen and the other at age twenty-five. I don't know how a parent copes with the loss of one child, much less two. I once interviewed Gerald Sittser, a professor at Whitworth College in Spokane, Washington. Sittser wrote the book *A Grace Disguised: How the Soul Grows Through Loss,* after a head-on collision with a drunk driver took the lives of his mother, his wife and a young daughter. "I lost my past, my present, and my future," Sittser said, explaining the violent grief that knocked him around.

The one thing all these people have taught me is that perseverance isn't about our strength — it's about our frailties. Our faith is as tenuous as an endangered plant clinging to a steep ravine. If we are to survive the threats at all, we must root ourselves deeper, believing and trusting in the goodness of the one who made us. Perseverance isn't about our will. It's about God's will.

Just as the endangered trillium gives no thought to its precarious predicament, but simply goes about being the thing of beauty God created it to be, so must we stop our incessant worrying. If God has equipped an itsy-bitsy three-petal flower to survive on the cragged lip of a riverbank, surely he's not going to drop-kick us down a ravine, or smash our fingers until we cry "Abba, Father" and let go. We are the endangered species he sent his son to rescue, remember?

<< >>

The most faith-affirming book I've ever read (other than the Bible) is Dennis Covington's *Salvation on Sand Mountain*, about the community of holiness snake-handling churches.

Here's my husband's disclaimer about that and all other things related to me: "You're one crazy southern woman!" He does not understand my fondness for Covington's book. That's not a reflection on Covington's award-winning writing, but indicative, I think, of the night Tim went to shake me awake from a nightmare, and I slapped at him, hollering, *"Get behind me, Satan!"*

He happened to awaken me at the very moment I was sprinkling demons with blood. I think Tim's afraid he's going to come home some night and find me fondling a rattler.

Covington explains in his book that he didn't grow up tossing snakes on Sunday mornings, but became familiar with the holiness community as a result of his journalistic work. He'd covered the trial of the Reverend Glenn Summerford, who had been convicted and sentenced to ninety-nine years in prison for attempting to murder his wife by forcing her to stick her hand into a cage holding a disgruntled canebrake rattler until it bit her.

What captivated me most is the part of the story where Covington moves from detached observer of the rituals of the Church of Jesus and Signs Following to an active participant in worship, which includes coddling snakes and drinking strychnine toddies.

Covington and his wife, novelist Vicki Covington, were regular attendees at an urban Southern Baptist church in Birmingham, Alabama. Southern Baptists prefer the Holy Spirit move in a quiet, orderly fashion, like a dentist with an afternoon tee-time. They don't tolerate speaking in tongues, twirling in the aisles, or pitching snakes to and fro at the altar. If you want to see a Southern Baptist excited, buy tickets to the Auburn-Alabama game or the Georgia-Florida tussle. That's when they get rowdy enough that they might straddle a gator. Otherwise, forget it.

So you'd think a smart southern boy like Covington would know better than to mess with rattlers. But you'd be wrong. The people at the holiness church extended the hand of hospitality to Covington and his family, inviting them inside their homes, to their brush arbor meetings, to their church meetings. He went for the sake of research first, but then, as these folks befriended him, Covington began to identify with them. I don't want to spoil the book for you, but here's what Covington says about the day he picked up the rattler:

> This was the moment. I didn't stop to think about it. I just gave in. I stepped forward and took the snake with both hands. Carl released it to me. I turned to face the congregation and lifted the rattlesnake up toward the light. It was moving like it wanted to get up even higher, to climb out of that church and into the air. And it was exactly as the handlers had told me. I felt no fear. The snake seemed to be an extension of myself. And suddenly there seemed to be nothing in that room but me and the snake.[1]

The first time I read that, my husband and I were headed south on Interstate 85 out of Atlanta. He was doing the driving; I was doing the reading. I yelped.

"What?" he asked. "What's going on?" Tim thought maybe I'd seen another demon.

"This story about the snake handlers. Can you imagine picking up a rattler?"

"No!" Tim said emphatically, his dark eyebrows raised in suspicion.

"I think it would be such a powerful thing."

"That's because you're a crazy southern woman."

"No it's not. Imagine, holding in your hands for just a brief moment the thing that scares you the most. Wouldn't that be an incredible thing? To conquer that fear?"

"Not if it means putting my hand in a rattler box," Tim said. Then turning to the kids, he added, "Don't listen to your mother. She's not right in the head."

Our kids nodded in agreement and assured their father they wouldn't be carrying any snakes home for Mama to handle.

<< >>

I was in Vietnam when I picked up the mighty-muscled python. It was March 2003. I'd boarded a big ol' jet air-liner out of LAX and crossed the ocean canyons on my way to Ho Chi Minh City, which the native Vietnamese still call Saigon. The night before I left Portland for LAX, my brother Frank called.

"Are you going to Hanoi?"

"Yes, we're going all over the country."

"Well, don't expect me to come bail you out of jail if they arrest you," he said.

"No problem," I assured him. "I'm not the one with the criminal history, remember?"

My mother called too. There was talk of war. Of the U.S. invading Iraq. She couldn't help but worry. The last time she sent someone off to Vietnam he came home in a casket.

"I wish you wouldn't go," she said.

But I would not let my mother's fears or mine stop me.

I had not known all those years earlier when I sat on that front porch in Pendleton and asked God for the grace to overcome my greatest fear that I would one day board a plane for a *twenty-hour* plane flight! I could not have imagined it then, but God knew. He knew, and he was readying me for the journey.

I traveled to Vietnam along with a group of other adults just like me — sons and daughters whose fathers had all died in Vietnam. I recorded that journey in compelling you-gotta-read-this-honey detail in my book *After the Flag Has Been Folded*, so I won't recount it all here, other than to tell you about the day I picked up the mighty, mighty python.

We spent three hours on the bus, traveling from downtown Saigon to the Mekong River. We passed acres of banana, pod, and palm trees, and clusters of brightly dressed people everywhere, squatting on the ground or sitting in white, pink, or blue plastic chairs. Merchants peddled their goods on the backs of bikes — straw, balloons, baskets, and bowls. They did not flinch when the bus driver whizzed by and blasted the horn. Motor bike repair shops sprouted on every corner like Starbucks in Seattle.

The Mekong was as muddy as the Chattahoochee River in Georgia, and the weather not much different — hot and muggy. We climbed into the wooden pea-pod sampan and headed upriver, where we had a prearranged lunch date.

After a meal of fried elephant fish, pork, chicken, rice, rice, and more rice, our Vietnamese host walked out with a fifty-pound python draped around his neck and asked if anyone wanted a turn at holding the snake.

Now Covington's buddies at the holiness church warned him that a person should never handle a snake without prayer and prompting from the Holy Spirit. But this wasn't a brush arbor meeting, and the only preacher we had with us was a Catholic priest. I had no idea what his theological position on snake-handling was, but I knew one thing — I'd already held the things I feared most in my hands — the fear of flying, the fear of a people I'd long considered my enemy, the Vietnamese. A python was nothing by comparison.

"I want to hold him!" I hollered. Someone draped the creature over my shoulders.

I felt no fear. But then again, that wasn't a ginormous rattler wrapped around my neck.

Looking back now, I marvel at how much ground I've covered since that time, a whole heck of a lot of it by air. I understood from the get-go that my fear of flying was a phobia. And that prayer alone wasn't going to cure what ailed me. I was convinced, some might say convicted, that I'd been indulging my phobia. Allowing my imaginations to control me. Hard as it was to admit as a believer, I simply did not trust God. That Heavy Metal Jesus was still lurking in the dark, waiting for the moment when he'd most likely find me off-guard before pouncing and knocking me off my feet again.

Identifying my problem was easy enough. Fixing it

required some work. Let's say your best friend comes to you and says, "I don't have much faith anymore. Do you know how I could go about getting some?" What would you tell him?

Repeat it with me: "Faith comes from hearing the message, and the message is heard through the word of Christ" (Rom. 10:17).

Let me clarify something. I'm not suggesting that a person who suffers from anxiety, depression, bipolar disorder, or any number of physical or mental illnesses that can lead to dizzying delusions or paralyzing paranoia, can just commit Scriptures to memory and that will cure them. I am a huge proponent of seeking counseling and medical intervention as needed for such problems. Prayer helps, and so does studying the Word. But Eric Shannon is a classic example of all the things that can go wrong when a person fails to get the medical intervention necessary and when a person self-medicates as a means to deal with his own personal demons. Too often the self-medication becomes a demon of its own.

But for all the rest of us common pilgrims struggling along with our routine yet, nonetheless, debilitating fears, we have to make faith a practice. The most obvious way to start building faith is by committing Scripture to memory.

I began by meditating on the prayer of the father in Mark 9:14-24:

> When they came to the other disciples, they saw
> a large crowd around them and the teachers of the

*law arguing with them. As soon as all the people saw
Jesus, they were overwhelmed with wonder and ran to
greet him.*

*"What are you arguing with them about?" he
asked.*

*A man in the crowd answered, "Teacher, I brought
you my son, who is possessed by a spirit that has robbed
him of speech. Whenever it seizes him, it throws him to
the ground. He foams at the mouth, gnashes his teeth
and becomes rigid. I asked your disciples to drive out
the spirit, but they could not."*

*"O unbelieving generation," Jesus replied, "how
long shall I stay with you? How long shall I put up
with you? Bring the boy to me."*

*So they brought him. When the spirit saw Jesus, it
immediately threw the boy into a convulsion. He fell to
the ground and rolled around, foaming at the mouth.*

*Jesus asked the boy's father, "How long has he been
like this?"*

*"From childhood," he answered. "It has often
thrown him into fire or water to kill him. But if you
can do anything, take pity on us and help us."*

*"'If you can?'" said Jesus. "Everything is possible
for him who believes."*

*Immediately the boy's father exclaimed, "I do be-
lieve; help me overcome my unbelief!"*

<< >>

A trip to Vietnam may not seem like such a huge victory
to someone who has never suffered from a debilitating
fear, but for those of you who have, you understand what

I mean when I say a person has to practice faith. I could have prayed myself purple, but until I took a step out and boarded a plane, I wasn't practicing my faith.

If we live long enough, bad things are sure to happen. Parents fall ill. Children die. Planes crash. Bad guys blow up markets. Powerful men build bigger bombs and endanger everyone with their silly war games.

The constant click of threat ticks through our minds as we consider the ever-growing list of enemies we face. Keeping up with enemies is exhausting work. We've been led to believe that the biggest threat evildoers pose to us is physical death, but isn't the greater danger what they take from us each moment that we live?

In his book, Covington noted that eight thousand people are bitten by poisonous snakes each year in the U.S. Only a dozen or so die. Good odds, unless you're one of the dozen. At the time Covington documented it, seventy-one people in the U.S. had been killed by poisonous snakes during religious services.

While I don't begin to understand or even want to understand, for that matter, why snake-handling or drinking strychnine ought to be a form of worship, I do marvel over the thought of picking up the thing that I fear most and grasping it, oh-so briefly, with both hands. To have even fleeting control over our fear is exhilarating. The captor freed is able to live a life more abundantly.

Where's your Jesus now?

See the fellow with the snakes?

Yep. That's him. Dancing.

Won't you join him?

GRAND POOBAH
of Conservative Americans

DESTRE LIVAUDAIS WAS FIVE YEARS OLD WHEN HIS FATHER, Staff Sgt. Nino Livaudais, was killed in Iraq in April 2003. Destre's younger brother, Carson, was three. Jackie Livaudais, twenty-two, was five months pregnant. When their mother told the boys their father was dead, Destre pondered the news, then told the Army Chaplain present not to worry because their father was in heaven.

"Heaven is a better place. There's no hate and no wars," Destre said.

A vision of heaven can be comforting to people like Destre and me, kids who've lost fathers to war. Destre and I long to live in place void of hate and its shadow, violence.

Despite our age difference, Destre and I have become good friends over the years. I've been to his house. He's been to mine. On school breaks, Destre, Carson, and their younger brother, Grant, come to Oregon to hang out. During one such visit, we hiked the paths at Mc-Nary Dam and searched for jackrabbits in the brush. We watched in an eye-glinting daze as Caspian terns and white pelicans fed near the pounding waters of the Columbia River. We wandered through a grove of towering pines, our steps silenced by the cushion of soft needles. And we raced from boulder to boulder to see who could run the fastest. I lost every time.

We cooked hamburgers and wieners on the grill while the boys dug a four-foot-by-four-foot hole in my garden, just to be digging. We colored Easter eggs with my daughter Konnie, and then she hid them in the backyard for the boys to find. And every single time Tim walked out of the room, Grant cried for him. Sometimes, after I read the boys a bedtime story or said prayers with them, my heart ached so much I couldn't breathe.

In the Livaudais boys I see the loneliness that comes with growing up fatherless. I know how much the boys miss their daddy, because I still miss mine. And I hope like heck that these boys aren't growing up without their daddy because our nation's decision makers got a wild hair for revenge.

I pray for our leaders. I pray for our troops. I pray for the Iraqis and their sons and daughters. I even pray about my sour attitude, but I'll confess I have a hard time with people who think they are generals in the Lord's army. Does anyone really believe God is a Republican and that he keeps a throne room at the Pentagon? Do people really think America is one nation under God, the only nation under God?

Forgive the digression.

At the end of the week, as I drove the boys back to Boise to meet their mama, Destre and I got to talking. His brothers were both asleep. When I first met Jackie and the boys, the family lived in Alabama. They moved to Utah after Nino died.

"Do you tell the other kids at school that your father died in Iraq?" I asked.

"No," Destre said.

"How come?"

"Well, first of all it makes me sad to talk about my daddy."

"Yeah. I understand that," I said.

"I know you do," Destre replied. He had made a pencil drawing of our fathers that hangs in my office still. When he gave it to me, Destre explained the drawing, "You were nine when your father died. I was five. That means you had your father four more years than me, but that doesn't really matter because they are both American heroes." And across the bottom of his drawing, Destre wrote: "I and my friend Karen Dads past away in a war."

"So what's the second reason you don't tell the kids about your father?" I asked.

"Because they think it's cool if your dad dies in a war," Destre answered. "But I know it's not cool. It hurts."

Destre Livaudais is hands-down one of the smartest people I have met in my life. His wisdom and insight silence me. I didn't speak for hours after that remark.

Destre went back to reading his Calvin & Hobbes book, until he, too, nodded off.

If Destre is right, if we are raising up a generation of boys and girls who think that it is cool to die in war, how do we then differ from those we now call our enemies? Could it be that we are creating a nation of young jihadists? Children who've been taught that there is no greater honor than to sacrifice their lives for their country? Children who have watched military heroes being lauded on national news and heralded in the streets of Washington, DC, and Greenville, South Carolina. Children who may indeed think the coolest thing in the world is to be blown up.

<< >>

Dr. Greg Spencer is professor of communications at Westmont College in Santa Barbara, California. Spencer has spent a great deal of time pondering the metaphors we use in the faith community.[1]

Spencer says, "We may not like to admit it, but we are a militant culture. If you listen to the dominant metaphors in a society, you find out what counts, and we use a lot of military metaphors because in our culture military matters."

Our language reflects that. Candidates camps "face-off" or "square-up." Corporations stage "hostile take-overs." Homeowners find themselves "wiped-out," "defeated." We declare war on poverty, war on drugs, and even war on domestic violence. How incongruent is that? A public service built on a mentality that says, "Let's slaughter them before they kill us."

Our schools are rivals, arch-enemies who have to "battle it out" on the football field, the baseball field, or in the school parking lots. We align ourselves by "choosing sides" in the classroom, on the playground, in the neighborhood — The Bloods and the Cripps — and in the political arena — Liberals and Conservatives.

Whether we are speaking about a ball game, a court case, or even our theology, we frame everything around our affinity for duking it out. At church, we teach our children sword drills and battle songs — "I'm in the Lord's army, yes, sir!" And we encourage each other to be "armed and ready for battle." Even our attempts at peace come about through "marching," "campaigns," "demonstrations," and "protests."

"The church has an affinity for war rhetoric," Spencer said. "There's a lot of doom-saying in our culture. It's part of the eschatology of the church. Many think that some sort of military showdown between Christians and Muslims is inevitable. In a perverse way, many are rooting for this destruction."

It is the same age-old wearisome rhetoric of "us" against "them." It's the way we think in the good ol' U.S. of A. We believe we are the lone defenders of righteousness, law, and truth. Anyone not with us is against us. They are our enemies. They are evil. They must be defeated. They must be destroyed. They must be obliterated. Is it any wonder so many fundamentalists have been strident in their support of this current war?

"The Iraq War? Who cares?" Spencer said. "It's all part of the Middle East Armageddon."

Fear has long been a strong element of faith for the fundamentalists and an equally strong element of fire-and-brimstone evangelism: Be saved or burn, baby, burn. Such an approach underscores our inability to change anything in our world — so why try? Why be good stewards of the earth if it is just going to be blown to smithereens anyway? No need to try and befriend our Muslim neighbor since they are the enemy of Christ, all terrorists in the making.

"Fundamentalists live out a heritage of a reactionary faith, instead of acting out of hope for a changing culture," Spencer said. "That kind of approach is pathetic. It keeps us from taking action."

Rather than standing up as a witness to hope or a prophet for change, too often those who call themselves the faithful accommodate whatever society dictates, often spiritualizing it, and baptizing it. That's how we end up with the whole connection between the Christian Right and the Republican Party.

Fundamentalists always see themselves as under siege. They need religion for the power it provides, not the hope. They gather their strength by identifying enemies — there is always an enemy, and if there isn't, they'll make one up. Without an enemy, there is no fear, and without fear, there is no power.

These folks believe that the world is going to hell in your granny's hand basket, and if you don't want to be left behind, you better arm yourself and your family with the Word of God and a semi-automatic assault rifle.

These are the same people who stocked their basements full of toilet paper and gallon jugs of water and C-rations and then spent the week hunkered down, praying over their children during Y2K. Surely you remember the panic sweeping this nation on the eve of January 1, 2000, right? All those dire predictions of widespread power outages, bank failures, computer meltdowns? All those people hoarding cases of toilet paper and pork-n-beans seem a mite silly now, don't they?

The thing is, fundamentalists need to see themselves as pitted against the world. It gets their juices flowing, and it gives them a reason to hole up and hunker down. Allows them to continue their rants disguised as discourse in a militant fashion. Perhaps nobody is better skilled at divide-and-dismiss rhetoric than conservative commentator Ann Coulter.

Whether she's taking pot shots at Muslims, Democrats, or 9/11 widows, Coulter's primary objective is to distort truth, not seek it. There's a big difference between asserting truth and seeking truth, and Christians who support Coulter ought to be ashamed of the way they've confused the two.

Coulter's opinions are not based on studied facts, but rather upon what she asserts as fact. Her methodology of meanness is the same one we all learned in kindergarten — name-calling. Educated folks call it *argumentum ad personam* or the abusive form of *ad hominem*. It's a rhetorical tool designed to insult or belittle others as a means of making a point, or underscoring one's own viewpoint.

Like when Coulter implied that presidential candidate

John Edwards was a "faggot." Coulter's remarks about Edwards played to the fundamentalists during an address at the Thirty-Fourth Annual Conservative Political Action Conference in DC. Her cursory summation of the upcoming Democratic hopefuls included the following remarks as reported by CNN: "I was going to have a few comments on the other Democratic presidential candidate, John Edwards, but it turns out you have to go into rehab if you use the word 'faggot,' so I'm — so kind of at an impasse, can't really talk about Edwards, so I'll just conclude here and take your questions."[2]

Coulter gives conservatives a bad name. One they don't always deserve. Thankfully, some insightful folks had the guts to refute Coulter's abrasive hate-talk. Senator John McCain called her out on it. But when the *New York Times* twisted her arm in an effort to get her to cry uncle, Coulter responded not with an apology but with more careless taunts. She reportedly defended her remarks to the *Times* as a mere joke: "I would never insult gays by suggesting that they are like John Edwards. That would be mean."

But too many conservatives and far too many Christians continue to encourage Coulter's inflammatory methods. She's become the beloved pin-up girl of the Fundamentalist Right. They cheered when her book *Godless: The Church of Liberalism* shot to the top of the bestseller chart.

Ignoring the very Scriptures they claim to live by, these folks heartily applaud Coulter's sarcastic and twisted arguments, whether they be about public schools, abortion, the environment, or war.

"Most public schools are — at best — nothing but expensive babysitting arrangements, helpfully keeping hoodlums off the streets during daylight hours. At worst, they are criminal training labs, where teachers sexually abuse the children between drinking binges and acts of grand larceny."[3]

Or "The core of Judeo-Christianity traditions says that we are utterly and distinctly apart from other species. We have dominion over the plants and the animals on Earth. God gave it to us, it's ours, as stated succinctly in the book of Genesis. Liberals would sooner trust the stewardship of the earth to Shetland ponies and dung beetles.... The core of environmentalism is they hate mankind."[4]

And "Democrats are not particularly welcoming of folks who do not believe it is a Constitutional right to stick a fork in a baby's head."[5] Or that Democrat Congressman John Murtha is "the reason soldiers invented fragging." On and on Coulter's rants continue, all in the name of Jesus and in defense of conservative Christians like herself.[6]

There's no disputing that Ann Coulter has found a sizable audience, one that appears to be predisposed to a mentality of "us" against "them." Her following is comprised of people who consider themselves "the Right." These same people claim they are the only real true believers. They are the only ones who really care about America and all that it stands for — God, liberty, and the right to lambaste (or blow to smithereens) anyone who doesn't agree.

The irony of Coulter's approach is that is so far-fetched from the life Christ led. Jesus didn't go around calling Mary Magdalene a ho. Or accuse Pontius Pilate of being a godless faggot. Nor did he take up a sword and threaten to disembowel that smarmy traitor Judas Iscariot.

Jesus did not come to redeem a political system nor to establish himself as the Grand Poobah of Conservative Americans. He led the life of a servant and died a sacrificial death. He didn't spout hate-talk but instead told us that we ought to love our enemies. "You have heard that it was said, 'Love your neighbor and hate your enemy.' But I tell you: Love your enemies and pray for those who persecute you" (Matt. 5:43–44).

The purpose of rhetoric, as taught by Aristotle, was to ultimately win people over to the idea of doing things for the common good, not to brow-beat them into agreement. Yet, Coulter's rhetoric is designed to galvanize the like-minded, to give voice to people who see themselves as right-minded and others as wrong-headed, or to be more blunt, those who see themselves as faithful Christians and the people who don't agree with them as godless evildoers.

Aristotle taught that rhetoric is about more than an ability to string words together. Carefully selected words can make an effective chokehold, as Aristotle aptly noted: "Why do states honor courage more than anything else, though it is not the highest of the excellences? Is it because they are continually either making war or having war made against them, and courage is most useful in both these circumstances? They, therefore, honor not that which is best, but that which is best for themselves."[7]

What if my friend Destre is right? What if we are raising up a generation of American children who believe that dying for one's country is about the coolest job ever? How did we get to this point? And what are we going to do to reverse the damage done?

As those experts over at the holiness church warned Covington before he picked up that snake, you have to start with prayer. But as Oswald Chambers, the great Sean Connery of Christianity, noted, "We have to pray with our eyes on God, not on the difficulties." In other words, forget about the snake, forget about all that threatens us — look at God.

Those holiness people know who their enemy is — and it isn't the rattler. It is not liberals or conservatives. It is not Democrats or Republicans. It is not Jews or Hamas. It is not Iraqis, North Koreans, or even the French. Our real enemy isn't a person at all. It's a fallen angel, whose power can't be destroyed by nuking but, through prayer, can be denied. Paul tells us exactly how in Ephesians:

Finally, be strong in the Lord and in his mighty power. Put on the full armor of God so that you can take your stand against the devil's schemes. For our struggle is not against flesh and blood, but against the rulers, against the authorities, against the powers of this dark world and against the spiritual forces of evil in the heavenly realms. Therefore put on the full armor of God, so that when the day of evil comes, you may be

*able to stand your ground, and after you have done
everything, to stand. Stand firm then, with the belt of
truth buckled around your waist, with the breastplate
of righteousness in place, and with your feet fitted with
the readiness that comes from the gospel of peace. In
addition to all this, take up the shield of faith, with
which you can extinguish all the flaming arrows of the
evil one. Take the helmet of salvation and the sword of
the Spirit, which is the word of God. And pray in the
Spirit on all occasions with all kinds of prayers and
requests. With this in mind, be alert and always keep
on praying for all the saints.*

Ephesians 6:10-18

It's no accident that Paul hijacked military rhetoric to
get his message across. Paul had to contend with the far
right in his day, too. He knew their lingo. But instead
of encouraging us to strap on our six-guns and swagger
down Broad Street, looking for a fight, Paul admonishes
us to prepare ourselves spiritually.

This idea that we ought to build a mighty fortress at
Ruby Ridge, and stockpile the cellar with guns and green
beans for the coming tribulation is not what Paul meant
when he urged us to be alert. Since when did "be alert"
become code for Christians to arm themselves?

I live in a community where people hang rifles in the
windows of their trucks and stuff their glove boxes with
extra ammo, so I'm not going to debate the holiness of the
NRA, one way or the other. But I do think as believers we
ought to change our discourse about spiritual matters.

Instead of always talking in terms of battles and wars,

Greg Spencer suggested we ought to try using the language of dance. I bet if Hugo Chavez and Pat Robertson would hook up for a samba, they'd discover that they have a lot more in common than they'd ever imagined — like two left feet, perhaps? Imagine Hilary Clinton and Ann Coulter, donned in red sequin dresses, working out the cha-cha together. Their greatest challenge would be how to get in step with each other. Of course, there's plenty of evidence that Iran's President Mahmoud Ahmadinejad already knows how to waltz around the issues, but what if he and Columbia University President Lee Bollinger joined together for a pounding rumba?

<< >>

Every other year, in late August, the Hopi Indians prepare for their ritual snake dance. They build an altar, gather prayer sticks, craft paintings from sand, and fill bowls with sacred water.

The festivities last nine days. On the last four days, Hopi Snake priests go into the wilderness to gather snakes, taking with them the young boys of the Snake clan, who are believed to possess a power that allows them to handle snakes without harm. While the priests root snakes from their holes with a digging stick, young boys stand ready with feathers, used to tickle the snake, coaxing them to relax and not strike. Then the boys grab the snakes behind the head.

On the ninth day — the ceremonial day — the snakes are put in a jar of water, doused with special herbs, then tossed onto a bed of clean sand, where they are guarded by the youth until the priests come to gather them in a large bag. They are carried to the village plaza and placed in a cone-shaped shrine called a kisi. Later, during the actual snake dance, the priest will reach into the kisi and grab a snake, first with his hands, then in his mouth.

This continues until all fifty or sixty snakes in the bag have "danced." Then the priests make a circle of meal, and the snakes are tossed into the circle, as women and children sprinkle more meal on the squirming creatures. Afterward, Snake priests rush into the circle, gather snakes by the armloads and carry them off to sacred places to be released. Hopefully, some place far, far away.

The ritual is performed with great respect, but because the Hopi consider the snakes their "brothers," the dance is not considered dangerous. The Hopi believe the snakes will carry their prayers for rain to Creator. They end their dancing by drinking a vomit-inducing substance to purge themselves from any potential poisons.

The Hopi are not, as some believe, worshipping snakes. Quite the opposite. They have befriended the snakes as their brothers. They've managed to live with them, peacefully. They pray with them. They dance with them.

You'd think that if it's possible for man to befriend a bull snake or a rattler, that it wouldn't be all the difficult for us to learn to get along with each other. If only we had a season, or a reason, where we all could come together for dancing and praying.

Instead of equipping our children with six guns for the Late Great Shoot-Out, maybe we ought to get them some dancing shoes and teach them to mix up some moves. What would happen if we all quit fussing around so much, and strived more to get our groove on? We all ought to take a deep breath, poise ourselves and give Satan the Shim, Sham, Shimmy.

Fix What's AILING Me

I WAS SIPPING A CUP OF HOT COFFEE, WORKING ON A manuscript at the restaurant in the Cumberland Mountain State Park in Tennessee one summer morning, when I overheard some folks talking at the table behind me. Their conversation was like a poetry reading: Pauses were interjected only for the sake of emphasis. I quickly opened up a new file and took notes:

"Hey, you like my hair?"

"Yeah. You got that Farrah Fawcett look going on." (You know you're in the South when a Farrah Fawcett hairdo is considered a good look in 2006.)

"Hey Bea, did you hear the news this morning about JonBenet Ramsey? They done arrested somebody. Give his name on *Nightline* last night. Arrested him over in Thailand."

"They did?"

"So sad. Her momma's dead, ain't she?"

"Yeah, but I heared she knew they had a suspect before she died."

"Weelll."

"They thought she did it at first, didn't they?"

"Weelll, at first. But so did I."

"I did too."

"The parents are always the first ones suspected anymore."

"That Thailand is a sick place. I heared tell they sell their own daughters into prostitution."

"You don't say?"

"And American businessmen are going over there for that very reason."

"Weelll, that is sick."

"Did you hear about that boy that fell from the diving board this week?"

"Nah, Lawd. What happened?"

"I heared he was about eight steps up the diving board and fell on his head on the concrete. Got a skull fracture. Air was seeping into his brain and nasal cavity. Blood was coming out of his ears."

"Weelll."

"But the thing is, his momma and daddy didn't have no health insurance. They flew him off to some hospital in Nashville, but because he didn't have no insurance, he was home four days later. Can you believe that?"

"How do they get away with that?"

"I heared tell that they sometimes won't take a person ain't got no health insurance."

"What about that hypocritic oath thing? I thought they couldn't turn nobody away."

"They find a way to get around that."

"Weelll, I understand it. I work so my family has insurance. I don't think it's right that people ain't working get it."

"I see your point. Every story has two sides."

"They said Mrs. Sally had a nervous breakdown. Come to find out, she was out in her garden. You know that purple weed that grows in the garden?"

"Yeah. I got me some all in my garden."

"The one with the purple blooms?"

"Yeah. Yeah."

"Mrs. Sally was out picking lettuce and got some of that weed in her lettuce, and that's why come she to have that breakdown. That stuff's bad poison. Rare, but dangerous. One little fella, he got into it, and his muscle turned to stone. Ain't but twenty or thirty cases of that a year. The doctor don't see much of it. But you know, I got that stuff all up in my garden, and every time I go in my garden, I get nervous. I believe that purple weed is what's making me that'a way."

"Weelll."

Conversations like this one are taking place in coffee shops the world over. Talk of perverted American businessmen banging away on young girls in exotic places. Talk of accidents that cause families to fall prey to a villainous health care system. Talk of the threats that loom in our very gardens, where the kale, left to its own evil devices, becomes unhinged, attacks the unsuspecting, leaving folks stone-cold dead or crazy as a meth-fed beagle.

As if the news that CNN spews at us 24/7 isn't enough to keep our guts twisted like barbed wire, we have to go around ruining a good morning by telling each other every awful story we can think of in a fifteen-minute coffee break. It sounds like we're auditioning for a spot on *Entertainment Tonight*.

We've plumb forgotten that what we are supposed to be doing is *encouraging* one another. (Okay. The Farrah Fawcett hairdo remark was an encouragement of sorts. But if you have to fish for a compliment, then it doesn't really count.)

Remember 1 Thessalonians 5:11: "Therefore encourage one another and build each other up, just as in fact you are doing."

And Hebrews 3:13: "But encourage one another daily, as long as it is called Today, so that none of you may be hardened by sin's deceitfulness."

Or how about this admonishment: "Let us encourage one another — and all the more as you see the Day approaching" (Heb. 10:25)?

Back in the days of yore, when my children were in school and I was running the carpool every afternoon, they would climb in the van and within minutes let loose a litany of complaints.

"I'm tired."

"I'm hungry."

"You know what Roy did today? He flipped up my dress!"

"Well, we had a stupid sub in recess who put me on the wall!"

The ranting would continue unabated all the way home, until finally, I figured out a way to counteract it. As the kids climbed into Priscilla Previa (we named our vehicles) one afternoon and opened their mouths to begin their stereophonic moaning, I held up my right hand to silence them.

"We have a new rule. For every bad thing you tell me today, you have to tell me three good things that happened."

There was a collective gulp as all four kids swallowed heavy grumbles.

"But Mommmm," my youngest whined, "that's not fair!"

"Okay. Now tell me three good things," I said, smiling that wicked-mother grin.

Imagine what the headlines would look like if for every bad story a reporter wrote, he or she had to counter it with three good ones? Stories of American businessmen who forgo luxury hotels to buy books for underprivileged children? Stories of doctors who donate their vacations every year to help heal ailing people in poverty-stricken countries? Stories about celebrities who are making good choices? Or about people who didn't turn to stone while hoeing their neighbor's cabbage?

There's no question that these are troubling times. Maybe even the end of times. I don't know. I'm not a prophet. But I am a person who has grown tired of being manipulated by fear and negativity — whether it's coming from the headline news, the *New York Times* best seller list, the pulpit at the First Signs of Christ Forgotten, or simply from the corner booth of my own mental ramblings.

Many years ago one of my dearest friends was hospitalized with what us southerners refer to as a "bad case of the nerves." As far as I knew she hadn't brushed up against any purple weeds in the garden. Still, she spent six weeks in one of those highfalutin facilities where doctors perform cavity searches that have nothing to do with your teeth. My friend disappeared into a mute darkness. For one entire year, she did not call, she did not write. With her she took the secrets of our shared youth. I fretted. Would she ever again inhabit the place behind that vacant stare?

The answer came to me in a dream. I recall the details with the same aching clarity that I do the births of my children. Here's that dream:

I was on a pier with twelve men, a long-bearded dude, and a Coast Guard captain. The planks were gray, weather-worn, but steady, which was a good thing because the pier was smack-dab in the middle of the ocean. Not attached to anything, it seemed anchored from beneath.

Docked at the pier was the sorriest looking pontoon boat. The hull was made of lightweight metal, and there was a ratty canopy that gave the boat the look of a four-poster bed. As we were standing beside the boat, a powerful surge flipped it over on its top. The long-bearded dude grabbed hold of one of the posts and yanked the boat upright. I was gob-smacked, but everyone else acted as though that was no big deal.

This bearded dude then had a heated argument with the Coast Guard captain. They were fussing about an upcoming trip.

As best I could make out, the Coast Guard had been called in to help find a woman who had gone off in her own boat and gotten lost in a storm. The twelve men and the bearded dude were offering to take their pontoon boat out and assist the Coast Guard. But the captain said their search had been called off, due to reports of a bad storm front coming in.

"It's too dangerous," the captain said, his face puffing like an angry blowfish.

"I'm going," the bearded fellow said. "Who's coming with me?"

All twelve men hopped in the boat. I stood there, eyeing the dark clouds rolling in. Lightning was flashing. The aqua water had turned a smoky blue. I looked at the captain, then at the bearded dude and thought, *Well, if I was lost, I'd be hoping somebody would come in search of me.* So I jumped in the now very crowded boat, where I proceeded to pull out supplies from a picnic basket I was carrying and slapped together enough tuna fish sandwiches for everyone. (Every woman knows you can't save people on an empty belly.) Some of the twelve men helped.

The storm grew more fierce as we pulled up anchor and pushed away from the pier. "Aren't you worried?" I asked the bearded fella. "Maybe we ought to wait for this storm to pass."

"No," he said. "There's a lost woman out there who needs help. We are going to find her."

Okay, I thought, *but I sure hope we find her soon before we all end up dead.* I didn't say this aloud for fear of offending these men, but I was thinking it loudly.

Suddenly the bearded dude turned to me and said, "Don't worry. It doesn't matter how ill-equipped you think you are, as long as you stay in my presence there's peace. The storms of life will never overtake you."

<< >>

As soon as he said that, I sprang out of bed like a jack-in-the-box. I don't like people talking to me when I'm sleeping. It's annoying. And I'm always worried about what I might confess to when I'm not fully awake. But even in my gravy-brain state, I knew in that moment that my girlfriend was going to be okay, so I called her and told her about the dream.

She was too doped up to understand any of it, but that didn't matter. I knew that the message wasn't as much for her as for me: As long as I stayed in the presence of Jesus, I didn't need to panic about life's destructive storms. Jesus would keep me safe and at peace if I went about my job of helping those in distress.

Okay. I know this reads like something out of a script for the *Twilight Zone,* or *Medium* (for those of you too young to remember Rod Serling), and you're probably thinking that I should have joined my girlfriend for treatment, and maybe you're right.

I'm not suggesting that God spoke directly to me. I didn't hear any voices bellowing from a dark garage or see any glowing embers from the chariot of fire. It was more like an inspired video podcast of Isaiah 26:3: "You will keep in perfect peace him whose mind is steadfast, because he trusts in You."

The message of that dream is something that I have returned to again and again as I have witnessed the swell of fear threatening our world from all sides. And even now, when I am assailed by fears from within and without, I shimmy up the leg of God, and cry out for the safety of his embrace. It is there, in God's protective lap, that the panic that seizes me begins to ease off. Soon my tears turn to deep sighs, and then a calming rest comes over me.

Who is it you cry out to when you are most afraid?

<< >>

In 2002 Shirley Dunham died of breast cancer. Charles Dunham became the single parent of two girls, then ages three and nine.

"The youngest one grieves for Mom quite a bit," he said. "Sometimes I cry when I hear a song that reminds me of her. I can't believe she's been gone six years now. It seems like yesterday to me."[1]

This is not the life that Charles envisioned for himself. "Our time together was short — thirteen years — but

Shirley gave me so much more than I had time to give her."

He's worked hard at raising the girls the way Shirley would have wanted. The girls are good students and attend the small Baptist church that has been the Dunhams' home church throughout their ordeal.

The girls don't talk much about Eric and have little contact with their mother, even though she has completed her prison term. The only home they know is the one they've made with Charles and the assortment of farm animals, which includes a miniature horse that thinks it's a large dog, and a donkey.

Charles tries to make sure that all of his grandchildren understand how important his faith is to him, how important it was to Shirley.

It is his faith in Jesus that has carried him through all of this, Charles said. He remembers with a wry smile how Shirley testified to the presence of Jesus in her life — both when an intruder was pressing a gun to her chest and mocking her and, later, when she lay dying of cancer.

Charles has studied the events of the night his stepson Eric Shannon died.

"I have turned what happened that night over in my mind two hundred to three hundred times," he said. "If it had been anybody else, I know I would have been more aggressive, but since it was Eric, I just didn't have it in me."

Charles is no stranger to violence. A Vietnam veteran, he spent three months running suicide missions along the DMZ. But Charles, who had hooked up with Shirley later in life, knew how much she loved her sons. So when Eric burst into the couple's bedroom that night, brandishing a semi-automatic assault rifle, screaming at them to "Give me my son," Charles tried to explain to Eric that his son wasn't there and that they didn't know where the state's child protection agency had placed his boy.

Eric wasn't buying it. He shot his stepfather and left him for dead.

"We didn't know where the boy was," Charles explained. "Children's Services was afraid something like this might happen, so they never told us where the boy was."

Charles, who would eventually undergo five surgeries on his leg, was in the emergency room when word came that Eric had been killed.

"I'll never forget that," he said. "They told me that I could rest easy now. But how was I supposed to rest? Eric was dead. It was the worst night of my life. Worse than anything I experienced in Vietnam."

Those who loved Eric best believe that desperation propelled him on that deadly mission.

"I've thought about it a lot," Charles said. "I'm not sure that I wouldn't have done the very same thing if somebody had taken my kids from me."

When Charles studies the events unfolding in the world today, he can't help but be reminded of the 1960s, when he was a young man headed off to fight in another one of our country's hotly debated wars.

"When I came home, I told people that the Viet Cong wasn't my enemy," Charles said. "My government was."

It is not a popular message to suggest the government exploited young soldiers, then, or now, but Charles has never been one to care much about doing the popular thing. He's a man of a strong character and a straightforward faith. A faith that assures him that in the midst of the most frightening experiences of our lives Jesus is right here, grasping onto us. If it had not been for that faith, for the steadfast love of Jesus, Charles said, he doesn't know how he would have managed.

If faith in Creator God is to serve mankind at all, at the very least, shouldn't it give us hope? Shouldn't it urge us to love others more? And make us more tolerant, more forgiving of ourselves and others? If faith is to be of any help to us, surely it ought to take the ugly aggression out of us, the way Charles's love for Shirley and Eric did him.

It seems to me that a faith without forgiveness, without love, without redemption, is nothing more than a set of rules by which we seek to gain power over others. That kind of man-made religion, that religion of Certainosity, fashions God into a pissed-off father, dropping shell casings on our head as we cower under a sleeping bag on the floorboard, weeping in fear.

That's the kind of religion Lila's father clung to when he prayed for an end to his daughter's rebellious ways and believed God mowed her over with a train. It's the kind of religion Eric touted when he handed a belt to his son and told him he had dominion over his sisters. It's the sort of religion that fueled the frenzy of the 9/11 terrorists. And it's the sort of religion that makes fundamentalists — Christian, Islamic, or otherwise — believe they are all right and all others are wrong. It's the religion of Certainosity that longs for the great apocalyptic showdown on the Late, Great Planet Earth. And, sadly, the people who embrace it are more than willing to die for the chance to say, "I told you so."

If our hope in Jesus doesn't compel us to be considerate caretakers of this good earth and each other, if it doesn't give us strength to overcome our fears, or provide us a calm in the midst of life's worst storms, the way it did for Shirley and Charles, what good is it?

What about you? If an intruder storms into your home and threatens your family, what will you answer when he presses a gun to your chest and demands, "Where's your Jesus now?"

Will you be able to answer with the confidence Shirley had?

He's right here.

Acknowledgments

I KEEP A FILE OF NOTES FROM READERS BECAUSE WHEN I'm down in the dumps, their words encourage me. One is from Alexa Megna, a college student at California's Palomar Community College. Alexa wrote to tell me that her instructor was using one of my books: "I just wanted to say what an inspiration you are to me and all my classmates. You and all your family are heroes in my eyes."

Alexa's note is also a reminder that I need to thank the people who enable me to do what I do — the people who are my inspiration. I hope they tear this page out and file it somewhere, so on the days they get down, they'll remember this book is the result of their skills, their talents, their hard work, and their devotion. Many are like family to me. All are like Cosmic Heroes, swooping in with all their snazzy doohickeys and helping free me from a bad pickle.

Big hugs to Ralphie's daddy, Mr. Word Nerd, for your willingness to clean up my ginormous messes. And for doing it with heapin' amounts of good humor, keen insights, and a deft red pen. You're not only a good daddy, Andy, you're a skilled editor.

A loud yelp of appreciation to my word tailor, Becky Shingledecker, who gently steered me around the slippery spots. Big hugs to Mike Salisbury, Cindy Davis, Marla Bliss, Karen Campbell, Joyce Ondersma, Michael Ranville, Beth Shagene, Jeff Gifford, and the rest of the hardworking and skilled team at Z-town. I am particularly indebted to the graphics department for working twice as hard. Thank you. And to Lyn Cryderman for seeing a story in a single sentence.

Dudley Delffs, thank you for bringing that good ole Vol energy and devotion to this book. I count it an honor to work with another who hails from the hills where my faith was first formed.

Thanks also to Scot McKnight, Janis Owens, Michael Morris, Sandra King, Patti C. Henry, Jeannette Walls, Bob Welch, and others in the tribe of writers. You all inspire me by the way you live and write. Also, much thanks to Wanda Jewell and all those faithful booksellers from Powell's to Page & Palette who struggle to remain independent. You do us all proud.

To Tim, for learning me and our brood big words and gifting us with big love.

Charles, you are doing a remarkable job. I pray God continues to use the legacy of Shirley's faith and your devotion to strengthen the multitudes.

To Peggy Stoneman Wright, for her unflappable grace, ancient wisdom, enduring friendship, and beach weekends.

A misty-eyed thanks to the Comm students at Central Washington University and to Chairman Lois Breedlove for welcoming me to the Ellensburg campus and for gifting me with challenging discourse. You all made me think — twice.

Thank you to Sonny Brewer and Southern Writers Reading for laughing, and groaning, in all the right places. And a bouquet of stargazer lilies to Shari Smith for laughing the loudest. Thanks, too, to the Fairhope Center for the Writing Arts, Miz Betty Jo, and all the other good people in Fairhope, Alabama, for all the many kindnesses you extended to me.

Lastly, but only because I'm hoping readers will remember this thanks best, a big ol' Georgia Bulldog whoop and holler to Stan Gundry. He knows why.

Notes

Chapter 1: Night of Terror

1. Account taken from reporter's notes, interviews, and the article, "Night of Terror: The Fatal Mission of Eric Shannon, One Year Later," by Karen Zacharias. *East Oregonian,* January 1999.

2. C. S. Lewis to Mrs. Frank Jones, *Letters of C. S. Lewis* (Harcourt, Brace & Jovanovich, 1966), 210.

Chapter 2: Feasting on Fear

1. Associated Press, "Police on Trial over Beslan Massacre," *Guardian Unlimited,* March 16, 2006.

2. Peter Finn, "Beslan Massacre Probe Defends Russian Forces," *Washington Post,* December 23, 2006.

3. Neda Ulaby, "Extreme Horror: Basic Escapism or Simply Base?" National Public Radio, *Weekend Edition,* June 9, 2007.

4. Kevin Sack, "Apocalyptic Theology Revitalized by Attacks," *New York Times,* November 23, 2001.

Chapter 4: Love Derailed

1. Lila is not her real name.

Chapter 5: The Religion of Certainosity

1. American Nurses Association, Continuing Education. *Menopausal Health*. "Safety Issues and Long-term Benefits of Hormone Replacement Therapy," 2000.

Chapter 6: Up in Smoke

1. Associated Press, "Pat Robertson Warns of Terrorist Attack in '07," MSNBC, January 2, 2007, http://www.msnbc.msn.com/id/16442877/.
2. Pat Robertson, Wikiquote, the *700 Club*, January 21, 1993.
3. Joseph L. Galloway, "Bush Mantra: Be Afraid, Very Afraid," *The Huffington Post*, June 8, 2007.

Chapter 7: John & Jabir

1. Jon Cohen, "Poll: Americans Skeptical of Islam and Arabs," *ABC News*, March 8, 2006, http://abcnews.go.com/US/story?id=1700599.

Chapter 8: All the Same but Differently

1. Fernando Ortega, interview for *Power for Living* (Colorado Springs: David C. Cook Communications, 2007).
2. Eddy is not his real name.

Chapter 9: Like Falling Snow

1. Daniel Tammet, *Born on a Blue Day: Inside the Extraordinary Mind of an Autistic Savant* (New York: Free Press, Simon & Schuster, 2007), 1–12.

Chapter 10: Exacting Revenge on God

1. Some information about these events is taken from various AP and news stories.
2. "CityNews: Motive Behind School Shooting and Part of Suicide Note Revealed," *CityStaff*. October, 3, 2006.
3. "Families Bid Farewell to Shooting Victims," CBS3.com, Oct. 5, 2006, http://cbs3.com/topstories/Lancaster.County.Nickel.2.303593.html.
4. Quoted in Jon Hurdle, "Amish Donate Money to Widow of Schoolhouse Gunman," Reuters, September, 12, 2007, http://www.reuters.com/article/domesticNews/idUSN1229970820070913.

5. Toby Keith, "Courtesy of the Red, White and Blue," *Unleashed* (Nashville: SKG Music Nashville, LLC, 2002).

6. "Amish Report Statement," WGAL.com. September 12, 2007, http://www.wgal.com/news/14100330/detail.html.

7. Joanna Walters, "Massacre That Still Haunts the Amish," *Daily Express*, October 1, 2007.

8. Hubert & Lillian Champion, interview by author. Pine Mountain, Georgia. 2007.

Chapter 11: Fear Transcended

1. L. Gregory Jones, email correspondence with author. March, 2007. Jones quotes from the NASB.

2. Desmond M. Tutu, "Are We Ready to Forgive?" interview by Anne E. Simpkinson, BeliefNet.com, 2001, http://www.beliefnet.com/story/88/story_8880_1.html.

3. Sean Smith, "My Happiness Is True Revenge," *Newsweek* web exclusive, June 16, 2007.

Chapter 12: A Life of Intention

1. Judy Woodruff, "Experiencing Other Faiths to Find One's Own," National Public Radio, *Morning Edition,* January 12, 2007.

2. Dotson Rader, "I Have Faith in My Family," *Parade Magazine*, October 7, 2007.

Chapter 13: The Frailty of the Faithful

1. Dennis Covington, *Salvation on Sand Mountain* (New York: Penguin, 1996), 169.

Chapter 14: Grand Poobah of Conservative Americans

1. Interview. March 2007.

2. "Coulter Under Fire for Anti-Gay Slur," CNN.com, March 4, 2007, http://www.cnn.com/2007/POLITICS/03/04/coulter.edwards/index.html.

3. Ann Coulter, *Godless: The Church of Liberalism,* (New York: Three Rivers Press, 2006), 169.

4. Coulter, 4.

5. Coulter, 21.

6. In *Godless*, Coulter says she is a Christian. Coulter, 3, footnote: "I often refer to Christians and Christianity, because I am a Christian."

7. Aristotle, *Problems*, 27.5, 948a: 31 – 34.

Chapter 15: Fix What's Ailing Me

1. Charles Dunham, interview by author, May 2007.

After the Flag Has Been Folded

A Daughter Remembers the Father She Lost to War — and the Mother Who Held Her Family Together

Karen Spears Zacharias

A Woman's Story of Love and Loss

- A timely tribute to those who dedicate their lives to defend their country
- An inspiring story of triumph and redemption

Here is the story of a family left fatherless by a war that shamed a nation and left thousands of children abandoned. This is the uplifting tale of a poor Southern family trying desperately to regroup in the midst of absolute chaos. You will be amazed by the strength of one terrified young widow's strength to raise three very confused children, her entire family caught up in a distant war that made absolutely no sense to them.

After the Flag Has Been Folded is an amazing story:

- For every woman, daughter or son — American or Vietnamese — who lost a husband or father to that war.
- Of reconciliation between a daughter and her father, a daughter and her nation, and a daughter and the people of Vietnam.
- For a country once again touched by the uncertainty of war.

Softcover 978-0-06-072149-7   Note: Published in hardcover as *Hero Mama*

Pick up a copy today at your favorite bookstore!

HARPER PERENNIAL

Share Your Thoughts

With the Author: Your comments will be forwarded to
the author when you send them to *zauthor@zondervan.com*.

With Zondervan: Submit your review of this book
by writing to *zreview@zondervan.com*.

Free Online Resources at
www.zondervan.com/hello

 Zondervan AuthorTracker: Be notified whenever your
favorite authors publish new books, go on tour, or post
an update about what's happening in their lives.

 Daily Bible Verses and Devotions: Enrich your life
with daily Bible verses or devotions that help you start
every morning focused on God.

 Free Email Publications: Sign up for newsletters on
fiction, Christian living, church ministry, parenting, and
more.

 Zondervan Bible Search: Find and compare
Bible passages in a variety of translations at
www.zondervanbiblesearch.com.

 Other Benefits: Register yourself to receive online
benefits like coupons and special offers, or to participate
in research.